The Women's Guide to Golf

The Women's Guide to Golf

A Handbook for Beginners

KELLIE STENZEL GARVIN

Thomas Dunne Books
St. Martin's Press 🅜 *New York*

THOMAS DUNNE BOOKS.
An imprint of St. Martin's Press.

THE WOMEN'S GUIDE TO GOLF. Copyright © 2000 by Kellie Stenzel Garvin. All rights reserved. Printed in the United States of America. No part of this book may be used or reproduced in any manner whatsoever without written permission except in the case of brief quotations embodied in critical articles or reviews. For information, address St. Martin's Press, 175 Fifth Avenue, New York, N.Y. 10010.

Designed by Jessica Shatan

ISBN 0-312-25184-X

10 9 8 7 6 5 4 3 2

I dedicate this book to my father, Bob Stenzel, whose unconditional love and support for whatever I choose to do in life makes him a model for exactly what a father should be. Dad, no matter where I travel or what I do, I always feel that you are right there with me.

*A*nd also to my husband. Tim, you are one of the most generous people I have ever met. Thank you for always being there.

I love you both more than words can say.

Contents

Acknowledgments

Special thanks go to Jerry Freundlich for listening and not laughing at my idea; Pete Wolverton for being so helpful, and such a golf fan; Jeff Stewart for being such a huge help in every step of the book; Rich Barber, my agent, for being a trustworthy friend; Atlantic Golf Club for all of their support; my fellow golf professionals who have allowed me to listen and learn; and Jeff Blanton and John Andrisani for their help with the photography and their patience.

Introduction and Purpose

Part One

Introduction

My name is Kellie Stenzel Garvin. You probably have not heard it before. I do not currently teach any tour players or play on the LPGA (Ladies Professional Golf Association). I am a PGA and LPGA class-A teaching professional who teaches brand-new golfers every day of the week.

My grandfather was a PGA professional, my father a PGA tour professional, and my mother a good amateur golfer in Rochester, New York. In addition, my father-in-law is a PGA professional and my husband a PGA professional. I started playing golf when I was three years old.

I played my junior golf in upstate New York, with several small successes, including the 1982 New York State Junior Girls Championship and 1986 New York State Women's Amateur Championship. I attended Furman University in Greenville, South Carolina, and played on the Division I NCAA Women's

Golf Team for four years with many talented players. After graduation, I traveled the world with my great friend Kathy Hart, playing the international tours, including European, South African, Asian, and Australian. This was a wonderful experience. During this period I started working part-time for my future father-in-law at a private country club in Jupiter, Florida. Entering the PGA program as an apprentice and going through the educational series turned out to be a very rewarding experience. I fell in love with teaching others and sharing their triumphs with them.

Being a woman teaching a very high percentage of women showed me that their learning style was very different from that of men. Being comfortable in their situation and surroundings was of such a high priority that learning would not begin until this need was satisfied.

The number of women in golf is exploding. Over the years I have been teaching, I have also seen a vast increase in the number of young women taking up the game. I teach the members' young adult children on a much more regular basis than in years past. Golf is now looked on as the thing to do, rather than an old man's game. This is great! And also the reason that I think so many women are taking up the game. All aspects of golf for women are increasing, as indicated by *Golf for Women* and *Golf Digest Woman* being two of the fastest-growing publications in the world.

What makes my book different from the hundreds of other golf books is that it is directed at the large market of brand-new women golfers entering the game.

I paid special attention to the order in which I wrote this book. Students must have an idea of what they are trying to accomplish before they can learn. For example, they must know what a putter looks like, what a putting green looks like, and the goal of putting before they can learn to putt. I assume the reader knows nothing about the game.

I explain the goal of the game, discuss the different golf clubs and how they work, and progress from the small swings (putting, chipping, and pitching) up to the full swing.

The fear of embarrassing oneself learning the game of golf is large. As I have already mentioned, I see, especially with women, a great need to feel comfortable in their surroundings. My goal is to give each reader enough information for her to feel comfortable with her understanding of the game but not too much information so she feels overwhelmed. I promise the reader that with this basic knowledge, if she accomplishes each section in the order written, she will have a successful and fun learning experience.

The overwhelming majority of my teaching career has been with brand-new female golfers. I feel I have been extremely successful. I am very good at making the task of learning to play the game of golf very simple. The book I have put together is very basic. My being a female instructor who is very good with people, I believe, allows others to be very comfortable around me.

Throughout my teaching career I have been continually asked to recommend a book for my students to read. I have had some difficulty in answering this question due to the fact that in my opinion most golf books are too technical for a beginner and very few assume the reader knows nothing about golf. I assume nothing in my writing. I have researched the market to the best of my ability and have found nothing similar to my book. My students over the years have been crying for something like the book I have written here, and that is why I have put the time and energy into this effort as I have.

Purpose

The purpose of this book is not to impress anyone with knowledge or large golf words but to serve as a basic guide to a beginner. The ideas here are very simply written so as not to confuse the reader. Whenever possible, golf lingo is interpreted into plain English, so you can understand.

I have seen a great appreciation from the students coming through the golf school at the Academy of Golf at PGA National who finally understand what they are trying to accomplish because it has been explained to them in terms that they understand.

Basic ideas are used in each section. As you become familiar with the game, you may or may not want to seek more information on each subject. I have tried to limit the fundamentals to the most basic, to minimize confusion and keep students from overthinking. Golf is a growing game for women, and many times there is a fear to ask simple questions. If you do not know the answer, there is no such thing as a stupid question. When you first start the game, I always tell my students, it is impossible for you to do anything wrong. If you do not know how to do something, then you will learn. My goal is to present the information in such a simple format that golf will sound like the easiest game in the world to play.

This book does not include absolutes, but I make many general statements, once again to avoid overthinking. I do not spend a huge amount of time on the full swing, due to the fact that every student, and every swing, is so different that they require individual attention. Keep your golf as simple as possible, using these basic ideas, supported by the guidance of your golf professional, and I think you will enjoy a successful learning experience. Have fun!

Righties Perspective

I apologize to the lefties out there. Since this book is written from a right-handed perspective, you will have to switch the rights to lefts and the lefts to rights! Sorry!

Lessons

Part Two

Lesson 1
The Golf Course

The golf course may seem a far-off-in-the-future place, where you will not set foot for a long time. But it is helpful to understand the layout of the course to understand what you must learn. When I teach I like to put the pieces of the puzzle together as quickly as possible. Understanding the golf course allows you a look at the big picture, so you can figure out where to put the pieces.

A regulation golf course consists of 18 holes. There are generally three lengths of holes: par 3s, par 4s, and par 5s. The length or yardage of the hole, which will be listed on your scorecard, determines the par. For our purposes, a par 3 is a short hole, a par 4 is a medium-length hole, and a par 5 is a longer-length hole, which can often look like an eternity to a new golfer.

I remember playing a par 5 at Frenchman's Creek and burying my tee shot into a cork tree. After wedging the golf ball from out of the trunk, not being happy, with my playing partner laughing at me, I remember looking up and realizing that I had over 400 more yards to travel. This felt like a five-mile-long par 5 at this point.

To be more exact:

Par 3: up to 210 yards

Par 4: 211 to 400 yards

Par 5: 401 to 575 yards

Par is the score that an expert golfer would expect on a hole under normal weather conditions, including two strokes on the putting green. So, in other words, on a par 3 an expert golfer would hit the ball onto the green in one shot, on a par 4 in two shots, and on a par 5 in three shots, each allowing two putts for the computation of par.

Now, are you an expert golfer? It is probably safe to assume no, due to the fact that you are reading this book for beginners. So scoring par would certainly be fun but is probably not a reasonable expectation at this time, nor is it a requirement for having fun.

I remember watching my student Toby making her first par. She made a long putt on a par 3 for her par. She was so amazed when it went in that she went into shock for about 10 seconds. It was such a great moment for her, and for me as well. Sharing this with her was very special.

The specifics of the individual holes will be described in more depth in the next chapter.

Lesson 2
The Golf Hole

The most important component of the golf course is the hole, not to be confused with the cup. The cup, a four-and-one-quarter-inch hole in the green, is lined by a metal or hard plastic lining, sunk, by mandate of the rules of golf, at least one inch below the level of the green. The cup, the ultimate objective of the player of each hole, is marked by a flagstick, a pole about six feet in height, usually with a cloth flag attached.

"How in the world," a bewildered beginner might ask, "was it decided the cup would be four and one-quarter inches when six or eight inches would have spared people much frustration and grief?"

It was decided in the seventeenth century, when cups had no linings and all greens were sand. By the end of a day's play, the cups had become very uneven in depth and width, as players had swept the sand away to retrieve golf balls. One imaginative foursome,

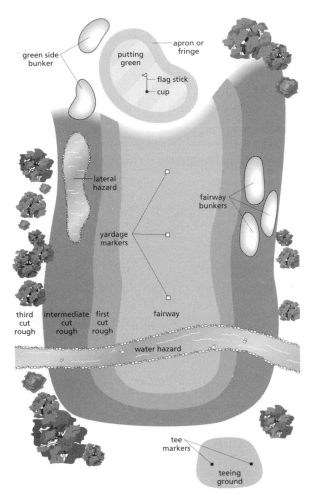

seeking to establish a more durable cup, spotted a length of drainpipe lying beside the putting surface. They confiscated the pipe and forced it into the sandy crater that the cup had become. A durable lining had now been installed. The drainpipe's size? Four and one-quarter inches in diameter, dooming golfers to an eternity of frustration!

There are 18 holes on a regulation golf course, consisting of several essential components. They are:

The teeing ground: The teeing ground, the starting point of each hole, is usually closely mown and contains the tee markers. Keep in mind that many of the ladies' tees, especially on the older courses, are aimed off center, steering you into trouble, or are very uneven.

The tee markers: The tee markers define the position from which the player must tee off. They are often marked with round balls or wooden slabs, which are color-coded for the different sets of tees. As a new golfer you should play from the tees that are the farthest forward or, in other words, offer the shortest yardage. Many ladies' tees are denoted with the color red, but not all, so be sure to consult the scorecard in an effort to look as if you know what you are doing.

You should tee your ball up in line with the two markers or within two club lengths behind the markers. Never tee off ahead of the markers. Beginners should look like they know what they are doing—the old "fake it 'til you make it" theory. So never tee off in front of the markers.

The fairway: The fairway is the mown area that extends from the teeing ground to the green. I had the privilege to play the ladies' South African Tour in 1987, and I never saw a fairway due to a very severe case of duck hooks. I think there were fairways out there. I should have put my driver away and just hit my 3 wood or 5 wood, but my stubbornness kept me from ever seeing a fairway.

The rough: The rough is the unmown or not closely mown area adjacent to the fairway. Rough can be cut on three separate levels. Adjacent to the fairway television announcers refer to the *first cut,* usually only a bit longer than the fairway. The *intermediate cut* is the second layer from the fairway. The mowers are usually set to a height of two or three inches for this cut. The *third cut* is uncut. This is where I spent two months playing from in South Africa.

Hazards: To challenge the player between the teeing ground and the putting green are hazards. Hazards include bunkers, which are depressions in the ground that may be either grass-covered or filled with sand, and water hazards, which may be creeks, rivers, dry waterways, lateral hazards, or simple water hazards.

- *Fairway bunker:* A fairway bunker is a depression in the ground filled with sand or covered with grass that is more than 30 yards away from the green.

- *Green side bunker:* A green side bunker is a depression in the ground filled with sand or grass that is located 30 yards or less from the green.

- *Lateral water hazard:* Lateral water hazards, which are marked with red stakes, are so designated where it is geographically impossible to go to the other side of the hazard in an effort to drop the ball to the point where you keep the point where the ball last crossed the margin of the hazard in between yourself and the hole. For example, the Pacific Ocean parallels the eighteenth hole at Pebble Beach. (If you ever have the opportunity to travel to play Pebble Beach, do so. I was fortunate to be able to play Pebble in a college tournament and more recently with a member of a club where I work. It is truly spectacular. It does not matter what you score, just truly enjoying the scenery. This is what golf is meant to be.) To help remember that a lateral hazard is marked with red stakes, keep in mind that the word *lateral* has the letter *r* in it for "red."

• *Water hazard:* Water hazards other than lateral ones are marked with yellow stakes.

Putting green: The putting green is the shortest cut of grass, which contains the cup and the flagstick. The ultimate goal of the new golfer is to get to the putting green. There is often a feeling of needing to be able to get to the green first, and then you will learn the short game. Once you are able to get there, you will then realize the importance of the short game.

The apron: The apron is a slightly longer cut of grass that encircles the putting green. It can also be called the fringe. This is the only kind of apron I have ever heard of. Is there any other?

Yardage markers: Many golf courses contain yardage markers, which tell you how far, in yards, the marker is from the center of the green. A yardage marker can be a plate in the ground or a bush on the side of the fairways. Keep in mind that it is measured to the center of the green, unless otherwise noted on your scorecard, so it will be necessary to add or subtract yardage if the flag is either in the front or the back of the green, in an effort to choose the correct club.

Lesson 3
The Goal of the Game

The Game of Golf

The goal of the game of golf is to advance the ball with your golf clubs from the teeing area provided on each hole to the putting green and into the cup provided on each hole in as few strokes as possible. There are 18 holes on a regulation golf course; therefore, you will attempt to do this 18 times. So, in other words, I have to teach you to get from here to there in the fewest number of strokes possible.

The Game of Golf for New Women Golfers

For most new women golfers whom I teach, their goals seem to me to be different from the goal stated previously. Their goals are to play a respectable game of golf, to avoid embarrassment, and to enjoy their time outdoors with their friends. These sound like great goals to me! The more lady golfers I see, some through our Women Teaching Women clinics at PGA National, the more I realize this to be true. The ladies just want to have a good time, to see the ball airborne and forward, and to enjoy the company, the challenge, and the location.

Lesson 4
The Equipment and the Yardage Chart

LESSON GLOSSARY

Loft: Also known as the angle of incidence, the upward angle of the club face, which determines the trajectory of the ball flight. A magnet on the face of the club clearly shows the loft.

Scoring lines: Grooves in the face of the club designed to give traction to the golf ball, so it spins backward off the club face (backspin).

Grip (club): Area of the golf club at the end of the shaft opposite the club head, designed for holding the club; wrapped with a leather

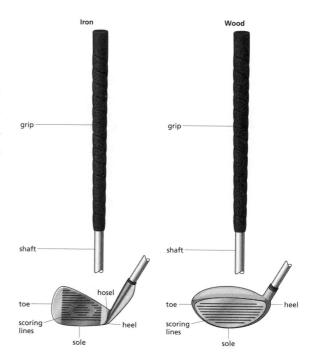

Iron   Wood

grip — grip

shaft — shaft

toe — toe — heel
hosel
scoring lines — heel — scoring lines
sole — sole

or more often a composition material to facilitate holding the club.

Grip (golfer): The process of placing the hands on the club; verb: to place the hands on the club.

Hosel: The heel or the neck of the club. Not where we want the ball to contact the club.

Shank: A shot in which the ball is contacted in the hosel.

Sole: The bottom of the blade of the iron club.

Toe: The tip end of the golf club opposite the heel or hosel.

The Equipment

Golf Clubs

Golf clubs have two major features that directly influence how far and how high the ball will go when hit correctly with each club. What you are looking at in the illustration is a full set of golf clubs, including the woods and the irons. Beginning on the left are the wood clubs (larger heads) numbered from 1 wood, 3 wood, 5 wood and 7 wood. Progressing to the irons (smaller heads), starting from the left, are the 3 iron, 4 iron, 5 iron, 6 iron, 7 iron, 8 iron, 9 iron, 10 iron (also known as the pitching wedge), and 11 iron (also known as the sand wedge). Note that there is a difference in length of one-half inch between each club in the set.

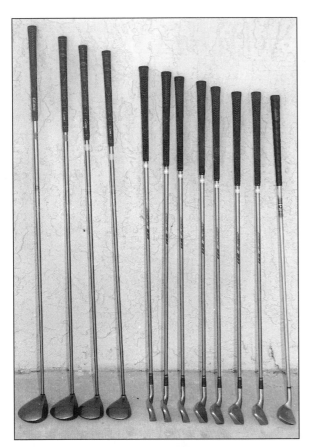

Woods on the left. Irons on the right. The clubs progressively get half an inch longer and the loft decreases by four degrees as you go from sand wedge on the far right to driver on the far left.

Remember from your high school physics class that the longer the lever, the greater the force? It's OK if you don't remember, because I am reminding you now. With a longer club, applying the same amount of power, you will be able to generate more club head speed. The result will be a longer shot. Going back to high school physics again, the loft of the club face will determine the angle at which the ball bounces off the club face. Picture the extension of the magnet on the club face as representing the initial flight of the ball.

To gain a graphic perspective of the loft, or slant, of club faces, set a tee on the face of the club, with the flat end of the tee on the face. For the purpose of illustration we have placed a magnet on the club faces of a 10 iron and 4 iron.

In most sets there will be a difference of four degrees of loft between clubs progressively through the set.

So, in other words, *the higher the number of the club, the higher the ball will go, and since the energy is going up, the distance the ball travels will be less. As the number of the club gets lower, the flight of the ball progressively gets lower and the distance the ball travels increases.* Also, as the number of the club gets lower, the club progressively gets longer.

The woods will generally travel farther than your irons if hit correctly, although you may have some overlap in distances between your longest irons and your shortest woods, especially with higher-numbered woods, like 9 and 11, becoming more popular today. Higher-numbered woods are also recommended for less-skilled golfers who protest that they hit all iron clubs the same distance,

The pitching wedge on the left will travel much higher and shorter than the 4-iron on the right, due to the loft in the face.

which is due to the fact that they are not applying adequate club head speed to exploit the difference in lengths of clubs. The built-in loft of the high-numbered fairway woods can help the newer golfer get the golf ball into the air.

Eventually you will learn the distance and within plus or minus a few yards you will be able to hit each club in the set. On the course when you see that you have a specific distance remaining to the green, you can select a club from your set with which you can hit the ball that distance. The ability to match distance to a club in your set will only be achieved after months of practice and experience. A yardage chart can also help you keep track of your distances.

Golf Balls

When you first walk into a golf shop you will be totally confused at the numbers of choices of golf balls with which you are confronted. Not only are there innumerable brands, but also within the brands there are many choices. But basically there are only three types of balls: the one-piece, two-piece, and three-piece.

A one-piece ball is molded of one material and primarily used as a driving range ball, where a particularly devastating hit splitting the one piece ball into neat halves does not make it a two-piece ball! A two-piece ball is constructed of a rubber core and a cover. A three-piece ball is a complex mechanism, made of a core of some sophisticated material, such as titanium, around which are wound many yards of thin rubber thread.

Golf balls have a characteristic called compression. When a golf ball is struck it is compressed, or squashed, literally, on the face of the club. The more difficult it is to compress, the higher its compression number, ranging from 80 to 100. Lower-compression balls are about 80 on the compression scale. These balls do not have to be hit as hard to be compressed on the club face.

There are two types of material used in the covers of balls. One, called balata, is a softer material, vulnerable to damage from mishit shots, but it produces a better "feel" for the player. The other material, called surlyn, is a boon to less skilled players because it is cut-resistant and not easily damaged by mishits. Balata balls easily develop what golfers nickname "smiles," gashes in the covers of the ball that look like smiles.

For beginning women players I recommend a surlyn cover, 80- or 90-compression ball. The packaging will include words like *distance* and *durable.* Don't choose a golf ball because it is pink or fuschia and is called the Flying Princess or otherwise appears ladylike.

The Yardage Chart

You will need to continually update this due to improvement or changes in the yardage you hit each club. It is important to remember that there is no distance you "should" hit each club, but you do need to know how far you do hit each club.

The charts here are examples. You will need to create your own with the help of your professional. Do not rely on your husband, boyfriend, or caddy to choose the appropriate club for you. The number of very independent women who will ask their significant other what club to hit in their playing lessons always shocks me. Be self-sufficient and use your yardage chart in your golf. Be as independent in your golf as you are in your life.

The maximum number of clubs a player is allowed to carry is 14, including the putter.

One of my most successful new students, and my friend, a really fun lady named Jeanne, took the yardage chart that we made for her, wrote the numbers down in her computer, made several copies of the chart, took them to an office supply store, and had them laminated. She then punched a hole in the corner of the chart, put a string through the hole, and tied the yardage chart onto her golf bag. She kept the extras just in case she lost the one tied to her bag. As a relatively new golfer, she always knew exactly what club to hit, and this took all of the guesswork out of it. This was a great idea. I wish I had come up with it myself.

(Measured in Yards)

PLAYER A	PLAYER B
11 iron, sand wedge: 40-50	11 iron, sand wedge: 30-40
10 iron, pitching wedge: 50-60	10 iron, pitching wedge: 38-45
9 iron: 60-70	9 iron 42-50
8 iron: 70-80	8 iron 48-55
7 iron: 80-90	7 iron 53-60
6 iron: 90-100	6 iron 58-67
5 iron: 100-110	5 iron 64-74
4 iron: 110-120	4 iron 70-78
3 iron: 120-130	9 wood 70-78
7 wood: 120-130	7 wood 78-87
5 wood: 140-150	5 wood 85-95
3 wood: 160-170	4 wood 90-98
1 wood: 170-190	3 wood 95-110

Lesson 5
Holding the Club

10-finger grip: The method of gripping the club in which all 10 fingers are on the grip of the club. Recommended for women with small and/or weak hands and for children. The 10-finger grip offers distinct mechanical advantages to a woman who has short fingers, weak hands, or arthritis in her hands. Children probably should be taught the 10-finger grip.

Overlapping grip: The grip in which the small finger of the right hand lies atop the forefinger of the left hand. Developed by British professional Harry Vardon, because his hands were so large that when he used the 10-finger grip his right hand was off the gripping surface of the club. The majority of golf professionals favor the overlapping grip. The majority of golfers who can't break 100 also use it; thus popularity is a poor criterion for choosing this grip.

Ten-finger grip.

Overlap grip.

Interlock grip.

Interlocking grip: The method of holding the club in which the small finger of the right hand interlocks with the forefinger of the left hand. The least preferred of the three grips for women, because two fingers are off the club, decreasing power.

The V's: The junction formed by the thumb and forefinger of each hand.

The word *grip* is probably an unfortunate term to use in reference to holding the club, as it implies force. The club should be held, not gripped. You will read or hear the expression "hold the club no more tightly than you would hold a bird." First, how many of us have actually held a bird? If you interpret that phrase literally, the club will probably fly out of your hands when you contact the ball. A certain amount of pressure is necessary to maintain contact with the club. But the pressure should not be so great that tension is evident in your elbows or wrist joints.

In placing your hands on the club, first set the club head on the ground. Your initial efforts at holding the club may be accomplished with any club in the set.

To align the club face correctly, set the club head flat on its sole or bottom so that the lines on the club face are perpendicular to your target line. (A target line is an imaginary line extended from your ball to your target.) Beginners are likely to have their attention drawn to the upper edge of the club blade, possibly because the upper edge is what you first view as you look down the club. If the top edge of the blade is aligned to be an extension of the shaft, the result is that the club face will be closed, or facing to the left.

Your left hand will be placed on the club first. Look at your left palm. Notice the crease in your hands that lies between your fingers and your palm. You should place this line on the left side of the grip of the club—not under the grip, but on the side. If you let your left arm hang naturally, you will notice that it is

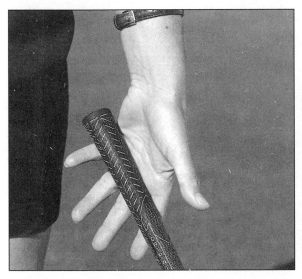

Place the crease between your fingers and palm on the side of the grip of the club.

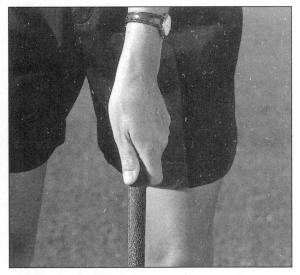

Close your left hand around the grip. The thumb sits just to the right of the center of the grip. You should see at least two knuckles.

slightly turned in toward your center, so your palm faces in toward your body. This is the way the hand should be placed on the side, not twisted underneath unnaturally. After you place this crease on the side of the grip, close the hand around the grip, so that the heel pad of your left hand rests on the top of the grip. Also, be sure the pad or the fat part at the base of your palm is about three-quarters to one inch down from the top or butt end of the grip. The underside of the club lies on the center of your fingers. As you look straight down on your left hand, you should be able to see at least two knuckles on that hand. Your thumb should set slightly right of the center of the grip, and the V formed between your thumb and index finger should point to your right shoulder. Your thumb and index finger should be close enough together to be able to hold a credit card in place.

Now, place an open right hand below the left hand so that your open palm is facing the target and the crease between your

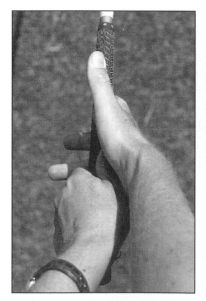

Place your right hand on the right side of grip so you cover the left thumb.

Close the right hand around the club. You should see one knuckle of the right hand.

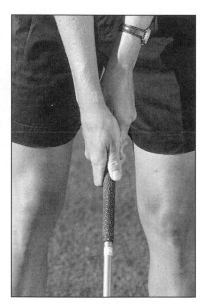

The hands fit together and work as a unit.

fingers and your palm rests on the right side of the grip. Then close the right hand around the grip so that the thumb of the left hand is securely and completely covered by the pocket formed between the two pads at the bottom of your right hand. You should be able to see one knuckle of your right hand, not your fingernails.

When you are going through the process of placing your right hand onto the golf club you will want to experiment with which of the two grips, 10-finger or overlapping, will allow you to put the right hand on correctly. Start with the 10-finger grip, where the right hand rests just below the left and the pinkie of the right sits on the club just below the index finger of the left. Then try the overlapping grip, where the pinkie of the right hand rests on top of the crease between your index and middle finger of your left. The grip that allows the right hand to cover the thumb of the left hand and lets your hands to feel they are working together is the one that is best for you.

Whatever grip you finally decide upon, the overlapping or the 10-finger, keep in mind that comfort is not a good criterion for what is right in golf. I have one pro friend who tells her beginning students; "If your grip is comfortable it is probably wrong."

It is absolutely imperative that your grip is correct. The grip is responsible for the club face at impact. A grip in which your hands are rotated too far to the right will tend to make the ball curve to the left (hook), just as a grip that is rotated too far to the left will tend to make the ball curve to the right (slice). If one hand is rotated too far to the right and the other too far to the left, you have a mess that will often cause the arms to collapse throughout the swing. If your grip is incorrect, you are going to have to compensate for it elsewhere in your golf swing. So to make your learning experience easier, work very hard at your grip initially; it will save you time and effort in the long run.

Avoid the Beginner Shovel

When you first are learning your grip, many of you will be hesitant to take your hands off the club once you have taken the time to put them on properly. A sure sign of a beginner is the beginner shovel. The beginner shovel, which you should avoid—remember "fake it 'til you make it"—is when with both hands on the grip you very awkwardly shovel a ball over from your practice balls and place it where you can hit it. Only reach for a golf ball with one hand on the club and then continue to practice putting your hands on properly. It is this repetition that is necessary to learn to put your hands on the club properly.

Homework

Practice putting your hands on a golf club at least 10 times daily. When your hands are on the club, use this checklist to determine if your hold is correct:

1. Can you see at least two knuckles of your left hand?

2. Can you see one knuckle of your right hand? And are you covering the thumb of your left hand?

3. Once you unfold your palms from the club and allow the club to rest on your fingers of both hands is the underside of the club grip across the centers of your fingers in both hands?

4. Is the heel pad on the bottom of your left hand resting securely on the top side of the grip of the club?

Expectations that the grip feel comfortable at this point are unrealistic. We hold no other implements—brooms, shovels, rakes, or flyswatters—the way we hold a golf club.

But Questions Linger

Typical student questions about holding the club follow:

> *Student:* The pad on my left hand is getting sore. Should it?

> *Kellie:* That soreness means you are holding the club too close to the end or not enough in the fingers.

> *Student:* My nails are digging into my palms. I've seen golf gloves designed for long nails. Should I buy some?

> *Kellie:* Those gloves won't solve your problem. They merely allow your nails space to stick out of your gloves. So your nails remain just as lethal as ever. The only solution is to file your nails down a bit—just a fraction of an inch should be enough. You don't have to sacrifice a nice manicure to golf.

Lesson 6
Setup

Setup (the position of the body in relation to the club and the club in relation to the ball) is one of the most important factors in a beginner's success in hitting the ball. If you are not consistent in your body positioning, it is impossible to hit the ball consistently. Now, you can carry up to 14 clubs, and as all your clubs are different physical lengths, how do you set up consistently? The one thing that will remain constant with every club is the distance from the grip of the club to your body. The length of the club will determine your distance from the ball. You will first set the club to the ball and then set yourself to the club.

Let's start with the width of your stance. This is important for balance. As a general rule, your stance should be between hip width and shoulder width: hip width for your irons and shoulder width for your woods. If you have any lower back problems and/or lack flexibility, you may wish to flare each foot out slightly to allow you to turn with comfort. After working with Mike Adams, an amazingly intelligent PGA professional and a very generous individual with his time and information, at the Academy of Golf at PGA National for the last three years I have seen what a difference this slight foot flair can make. It allows rotation of the torso to occur more naturally and also takes pressure off the lower back.

It is very important that when setting up, you bend forward from your hip joint first, before you flex you knees. Starting from slightly farther away from the ball than you will eventually be will

Your feet should be between hipwidth and no wider than shoulder width.

Bend forward from your hips, so your chest is over your toes.

help ensure that you bend forward from your hips to sole the club on the ground behind the ball. You will want to be very careful to set the ball in the center of the clubface. If you wish to hit the ball in the clubface it is very helpful to start it here. Be sure to set the club onto the ground rather than elevate the club head over the ground while you are setting your hands and your body. I often see players of all levels attempting to "guess" where to set their feet before they set their club or their hands. I call this the magic wand setup, because you just about need magic to set up the right distance if you try to set your feet before you set your club to the

Your spine should be straight, from your head to your tail bone.

ground and your hands to the club. We are not attempting to use mental telepathy with the golf gods but to have a routine that allows you to consistently set up properly to every club. When you bend forward from your hip joint, you should feel as if your chest is over your toes and your arms are hanging straight up and down from your shoulders, completely relaxed. Your spine should be straight from your head to your tailbone. As I place a club shaft on my spine from my head all the way down to my tailbone and bend forward, the club should remain on my head as well as my tailbone. Please do not sit back on your heels. Do not squat. In the olden days, we used to be taught to sit into a chair. I cannot tell you how many women have come to me telling me they have been taught to sit back into a stool. This is incorrect. For women, this will make contact almost impossible. Lean forward. If you do not, your swing will pull you off balance, away from the ball. You should feel your balance slightly forward with your weight on the balls of your feet. Keep your chin out of your chest. You should be able to fit a fist between your chin and chest.

Your arms should hang straight up and down from your shoulders, with your hands underneath your shoulders and not at a diagonal. This is where your arms hang naturally when you are bent from your hips, and they should return here during the swing. This will allow you to use gravity and centrifugal force to bring the club head back to the ball, rather than trying to use hand–eye coordination.

Your hands should hang directly below your shoulders.

There should be space between your chin and chest.

Your knees should be slightly flexed and should basically remain on this same level throughout your golf swing. You should feel as if your rear end is sticking out and never tucked under. This may not feel as ladylike as we have been taught to be, but it is imperative. You will feel very 'L'-shaped forward, with a straight spine.

You can check your distance from the ball quickly and easily. After you are completely set up, take your right hand off the club, opening your fingers, and wave it between the club and your body. You should have about an open hand of distance that might catch the grip of the club and your thighs slightly (about four or five inches).

I believe a good setup is more important for women than for men due to the fact that our centers of gravity are lower, in our rear ends. Unfortunately, if we squat at all or set into our heels rather than leaning forward, returning the club head to the ground becomes almost impossible.

Practicing setting up in the same order every time, will be very helpful in learning to repeat the same position. The recommended order is as follows: start from farther away from the ball than you will eventually be, bending forward from your hips to set the sole of the club on the ground just behind the ball, then carefully place your hands on the grip of the club properly, and finally, last but not least, step your feet to the point where you feel that your hands are directly below your shoulders and then slightly flex your knees, to relax and balance you. So in other words, set the club, set your hands,

There should be an open hand's distance between the grip of the club and your legs when your knees are slightly flexed.

and then set your feet. Club, hands, and then feet. The stepping of your feet is what finds the proper distance from the ball, as your club and hands should not be moving while you are stepping your feet. Using this same order every time will help you to be consistent.

Check and practice your correct setup constantly. Your setup will have a great influence upon your ability to swing the club correctly.

Ball Position

Your ball position in relation to your stance should change based upon the length of the club you are hitting.

> **Short to mid irons, sand wedge through 5 iron: Middle stance, or just barely left of center.**

Your ball position should be in the center for the short- to mid-irons. My stance is a little wider than normal to help you to see the ball position.

Long irons and fairway woods, 4 iron and 3 iron, 7 wood, 5 wood, and 3 wood: Just left of center.

Teed fairway woods and the driver: Ball in line with the instep of the left foot. *Note:* As the ball is in line with the instep of the left foot, the end of the grip of the club will be in line with the inside of the left leg.

Your ball position should be slightly left of center for long irons and fairway woods.

Your ball position should be in-line with your left instep for the driver.

Lesson 7
Aim and Alignment

I cannot tell you the number of women who come to me to tell me that they have trouble with their aim and alignment. I cannot tell you the number of husbands who come to me to tell me that their wives have trouble with their aim and alignment. Be sure to read and understand this concept.

Aim and alignment is the way in which you set your club face and your body to determine the intended direction of the ball. One of the most common mistakes is misalignment as a result of misunderstanding how alignment works.

Before you set your body you must set your club on the ground so that your club face aims at your intended target, your club face and the ball on the target line.

The common misunderstanding I have seen is the belief that if the line of your feet (the line across your toes extended on the ground visually) points to the target, you are aimed at the target.

To aim and align properly, your club face aims at the target and your feet are parallel to your target line, aiming slightly left of the target.

This is not the case, due to the fact that you will not swing exactly on the line of your feet but rather in a line parallel to it. Therefore, in order to aim at the target, the line of your feet actually has to be slightly left of your target. This is called parallel left. The line through your toes is actually aimed left of the target, but parallel to the target line.

Most right-handed players have a tendency to aim too far to the right, myself included.

A right-handed player aiming too far to the right will make compensations to correct this. The most common compensation I have seen is for the player to attempt to pull the ball left onto the target line, which can produce several poor results, including a fat shot (hitting the ground before the ball) or a hooked shot (right to left curvature of the ball).

Three recommendations for good alignment are as follows: First, always practice with an alignment club at your feet. I like to place two clubs on the ground parallel to each other so that the line down the middle of the two clubs is going to the intended target. Hit balls from the middle of the two clubs, keeping your feet parallel to the clubs. If you consistently practice with alignment clubs during your learning process, this will make your golf much easier as you advance. Jim Flick, who is a fantastic instructor and communicator and teaches for Nicklaus–Flick Golf Schools, has his students place an umbrella or ball retriever in front of the ball pointing to the target to help with body position, visualization of the target line, and alignment. What a great idea! This will take the guesswork out of your setup and allow you to work on the other aspects of your swing. Second, an alignment guide I use for my students, when you are set up to hit a shot to a target make sure your left shoulder is *not* in your line of sight. In other words, you should not be looking directly over your left to see the target. Your left shoulder should be out of your line of sight to the target. Your feet, knees, hips, and shoulders should also be parallel to the target line in order to hit straight, consistent shots.

Third, place your club across your thighs while you are setting up to hit your shot and attempt to make the extension of the shaft point just left of your target. This method is quick and efficient, and I have seen it help many of my students.

Lesson 8
The Waggle

A waggle is a "mini-swing" motion following the direction of your initial take-away. A number of good teaching professionals will teach the motion known as the waggle to intermediate players, even if not to beginners. I believe it is important to note that many good golfers waggle. I rarely have seen a poor player waggle.

The golf swing is made even more difficult by the fact that it naturally must be started from a dead stop. Overcoming this initial inertia can be accomplished by a waggle. Thus I recommend a waggle for a beginner as an "inertia buster" as well as to create a model mini-swing.

The waggle is subject to many variations on the basic theme. Carefully observe the professionals, both PGA and LPGA, in telecasts of tournaments. All players will make some sort of preliminary movement, most of which can properly be called waggles. The waggle is not a random movement; the waggle has a pattern. This pattern can be taught and thus learned.

The waggle establishes a pattern for the swing. The waggle is a mini-swing. The pattern is as follows:

Notice the waggle here is the same as my take-away.

1. **Back: With your hands and arms move the club head back along your planned back swing.**

2. **Forward: Retrace the path of the club moving back from position. Justin Leonard, a player on the PGA tour, is a good example of this.**

Helen Alfredsson, an LPGA tour professional, recently started elongating her waggle into basically a full backswing. She believed that she could not feel what she was attempting to accomplish in just a small waggle. I thought this seemed like a pretty good idea, though I wouldn't necessarily suggest it to my beginners, because it could unnecessarily slow you down. But it represents a waggle that is just like that of the motion Helen is attempting. I had the opportunity to play with her in qualifying school a few years back. She was certainly playing a different game of golf than I was. She hit the ball very long and very straight and with a lot of confidence. I was very impressed by her game.

Expert players skillfully and gracefully blend the waggle into the backswing. Following the inertia of the waggle by stopping the waggle defeats the purpose.

The waggle is an easily-learned antidote to "freezing" at the start of the backswing, an affliction suffered by many beginners. Ask your golf teacher to waggle with you; the pattern is definitive and quite easily remembered after a minimal amount of practice.

I've had the opportunity to play in several pro-ams during my summer months. One of the more common reactions of the amateurs to being nervous is "freezing" over the golf ball. They stand there for an excessive amount of time, and I can just about see the smoke coming out of their ears because they are thinking so much. Too much! The waggle or at least just a couple of steps with the feet could really help this. The longer you stand still, the harder it is to get moving again. Once you set up, take one last look at your target, look back to the ball, take your waggle if you wish, and then go.

Lesson 9
Pre-Shot Routine

L E S S O N   G L O S S A R Y

Target, intermediate: An object selected on a line toward the eventual target and about three to five feet from the ball (leaf, bare patch in the grass, dandelion, etc.). An aid toward alignment.

Target line: An imaginary line drawn through the ball toward the target.

A pre-shot routine is important even the first time you venture out onto the golf course. And I realize your first goal in this situation is probably just to make contact with the golf ball. It is common to see a new golfer set up to a ball and hit the shot, never looking at the target even once. I see this all of the time. But what a shame it would be to hit a great shot and end up in the middle of the water or the woods. Therefore, take the time to pick a target and learn to aim toward that target, so that when you do hit the ball well it ends up somewhere you can hit it again without a snorkel and fins.

Your pre-shot routine is the steps you go through before you take your golf swing, which put together your aim and alignment, setup, and grip. You must go through the same order of these steps before every swing in order to achieve consistency. I will give you a pre-shot routine that I feel produces very good results. This is the routine made famous by Jack Nicklaus, one of the greatest golfers of all time. It is also the routine that my father taught me when I was learning. You are always welcome to make modifications if you and your professional feel there is an order better suited to you individually.

1. **Take a practice swing. Your practice swing should be in your normal tempo, in a similar lie as the golf ball, and preferably facing the target, so you can be starting to focus on your target.**

   The purpose of your practice swing is to put your words into a feel. I may be working on taking my back swing straight back. When I take my practice swing I will be very careful to make sure that this occurs. When I go to hit the golf ball it is not necessary for me to think about this anymore. I will just attempt to feel the same thing I feel during my practice swing. This then makes it very important that your practice swing is realistic to the actual swing you will make with the ball. The practice swing should be the same tempo. It is very important that the club head hits the ground. This is necessary for the ball to get into the air, so I want to make sure that this occurs. Your preparation is the key to your success when you go to the golf ball.

2. Stand behind your golf ball, with the golf ball directly between yourself and the target. Your target should be something in the distance in the line in which you want the ball to travel.

3. Pick a spot visually on the ground in front of your ball so that if you were to hit the ball over that spot the ball would go to the target. A recommended spot is about three to five feet in front of the ball. This is called your intermediate target.

4. With your eyes, draw an imaginary line from the ball to the target, passing through the intermediate target.

5. Keeping your eye on your chosen intermediate target, walk around to the side of the ball in a position where you are getting ready to address and strike the golf ball. Set your club head on the ground behind the ball and the scoring lines aligned at right angles to the imaginary line drawn to the target. *Caution:* Particularly if the club you are using is an iron, be sure the lower edge of the club face is aligned perpendicular to the target line. The attention of beginning golfers is often drawn to the upper edge of the club face. If the upper edge is aligned perpendicular to the target line, the club face will actually be closed, or facing to the left.

Stand behind the ball, placing the ball between yourself and the target to pick your intermediate target. The lighter patch of grass in front of the ball is my intermediate target.

6. Bend forward from your hips to place your hands on the grip of the club and set your feet parallel to the target line between your golf ball and your intermediate target. If your feet are parallel to your target line, you are aiming properly at your target. Your hips and shoulders should also be parallel to this line.

7. Take one last look at your target to make sure you feel comfortable with your position and to refocus on your target.

This process written out may sound lengthy. It should take at the most five seconds. In simpler terms, the pre-shot routine is: pick your target, pick your spot (intermediate target), set your club, and set yourself to your club, with your feet parallel to the line between your ball and your intermediate target.

Try to take one practice swing in your routine. If you are having trouble making a practice swing that you are happy with on your first attempt, you can occasionally take another. It may be better, however, to take a few extra practice swings on the side while the others are hitting so that you do not slow the entire group down. Golfers who habitually take more than one practice swing not only slow the pace of play for their group but also wear themselves out needlessly. Develop the pre-shot routine, using the same steps, in order, for every practice shot, even on the driving range. Your routine must be the same on every shot, whether a full shot, putt, chip, or pitch. Your pre-shot routine must be practiced on the range to be able to successfully transfer it to the course.

Lesson 10
Putting

LESSON GLOSSARY

Apron: A closely mown area immediately surrounding the putting green. Although not as closely mown as the putting green itself, the apron is an area amenable to putting. Also called the fringe.

Breaking down (wrists): Permitting the wrists to flex during the putting stroke, particularly on the forward stroke. Not correct.

Lie: The angle at which the shaft of the putter is attached to the head. The sole of a correctly fitted putter should be flat on the ground when the player addresses the ball. You may observe some players, the Japanese star Isao Aoki being a noted example, who address the putt with the toe of the putter up in the air. This makes the goal of hitting the putt on the sweet spot of the putter difficult to achieve.

Putting: Rolling the ball with a nonlofted or slightly lofted club called a putter.

Reading the green: Determining how much break to play on a putt to allow for the slope of the green. Reading the green is both science and art. An enormous amount of practice and experience is required to learn to read greens accurately.

Sweet spot: The position of the concentration of weight in a club. If the ball is hit in the sweet spot of the putter, the face will not twist.

As the definition says, putting is the rolling of the ball with a club designed for this purpose, because the club head has little or no loft. Putting is most often restricted to the putting surface and its adjacent area, known as the apron or fringe of the green. Of the total strokes taken during a round, putts will constitute approximately 40 percent. If your putts add up to more than this, we suggest you make an appointment with your professional for a putting lesson. Consider that the top performers on the PGA and LPGA tours average about 29 putts per round! This is fewer than 2 per green.

There are several types of putters from which you may choose. A very distinguishable type is the mallet-head, larger in size, popular in many models on the tours. There are many shapes and sizes from which to choose.

You should start by choosing a couple of putters that you like the looks of. The first time I met my friend Terri, while playing the Futures Tour, she was putting with "the calico gal"—a putter with painted flowers on the back. I thought this was quite funny, but she did putt quite well with that putter. You might also look for a putter that has lines on it to assist you with your alignment. Take two or three chosen putters out to the practice green to see which makes the most putts, and also which reacts more positively when missed.

A putter with perimeter weighting is recommended. The extra weight on the edges of the putter will help putts not hit solidly in the sweet spot stay more on line.

Like your other clubs, your putter should fit you. There are a number of specifications to consider. Of these, shaft length and lie are most important. An average-length putter for a woman is about 30 to 33 inches. Most putters that are sold to you are 36 inches. A putter so long it becomes tangled in clothing or threatens to impale the player can be cut down to fit. Have the amputation done by an expert, who knows what length you need. A grip of the proper size to fit your hand is then installed.

The most important criterion for putter selection is that you like how the putter feels. No, the putter does not have feeling. You must feel the putter—its balance and its head weight. The putter should feel alive in its responsiveness, as I have observed, and enjoyed, with my new mallet-head, graphite-insert putter.

A friend who is a good golfer, probably a single-digit handicapper, has a putter that is too long for her. Consequently, to avoid entanglement with her clothes she moves the putter to the outside of her line on the backswing. My suggestion that she have her putter shortened was not enthusiastically received. "But I *had* an inch cut off," she protested. An inch was not enough!

The goal in putting is to roll the ball toward the hole, putting the ball into the hole in as few strokes as possible. The initial goal of the beginner should be to learn to roll the ball well. There should be no popping into the air or hopping of the ball. The beginner will need to develop distance as well as directional control.

Putting takes much less effort than the new golfer realizes. Almost every one of you will take a larger stroke than you need on your first several putts, sending the ball flying across the green. So your first several attempts are simply trial and error. Keep the tempo of the stroke smooth and even. Stroke your putts, do not hit or jab.

Addressing the Ball

Roll is easiest to achieve if you place the putter in the center of your body, with the ball slightly left of the center of your body, just in front of the putter face. Take special care to address the ball in the center of your putter face, so that the line on your putter will intersect the middle of the ball. Your eyes should be directly over the ball. You will stand much closer to the ball than in your full swing, due to the fact that the shaft of the putter sits much more upright out of the head than the shaft on an iron or a wood. You will still want to bend forward from your hips, to help you get your eyes over your ball. Your hands should hang directly below your shoulders, and your feet, knees, hips, and shoulders should be parallel to the target line. The sole of the putter, assuming the putter fits you, should be flat on the ground. If the lie of the putter is not right for you, it can be bent to fit by someone who knows what he or she is doing.

Putting varies drastically from your usual swinging motion in that there is no motion of the body during the swing. Only your arms and shoulders will move during the putting stroke. Your knees must be steady. Your head must be completely still. If your head or your knees are moving during your putting stroke, your putter face will open and close excessively, producing erratic results in distance as well as direction. We are limiting the moving parts to produce more consistent results. You can have a golf buddy put a club shaft next to your head or hold your head to prevent lateral movement.

The triangle formed by your arms and shoulders must remain constantly throughout the stroke. Any change in the angle between your wrists and your arms would indicate that you used your hands to stroke the ball, an action that will lead to inconsistencies. Your wrists should not break down. A tee placed in the end of the grip of your putter should maintain its position between your forearms throughout your entire putting stroke.

To avoid changing your wrist angles, the tee maintains its position between forearms on the backstroke.

And the forward stroke. Also notice the same length for the back and through motions.

On the subject of hands, how does one grip the putter? In the beginning, use a similar grip as for your other clubs, except place your thumbs on the top of the shaft (the flat edge) so your palms are facing each other. You will notice that the top of the grip is often flat, which will help you place your thumbs on the top of the shaft. You may later choose to modify your grip, such as using a reverse overlapping grip, in which all of the fingers of the right hand are on the shaft and the forefinger of the left hand overlaps the fingers of the right hand.

A practice aid in putting involves making a "railroad track" of two of your iron clubs. Place them close together and parallel, leaving just enough space so your putter head fits between them. This will allow you to practice keeping the putter straight back and straight through. The line through your toes should be parallel to these lines, so that your feet are perpendicular to the line of the putt.

To keep the ball on-line, the back of the left hand should stroke toward the target to keep the putter face square or, in other words, in alignment with the target.

The railroad tracks will help you take the putter straight back. Notice that my eyes are directly over the ball and my hands hang below the shoulders.

And straight through.

The length of your backstroke, which in turn dictates the speed of the club head, controls the distance of the putt. A good method of remaining consistent in your speed back and through is maintaining consistency of your grip pressure. Another technique to achieve even tempo is making sure your backstroke and forward stroke are the same length. Trying to accelerate consciously is an easy action to overdo, resulting in slapping, jabbing, or banging the ball. The stroke should be consistent in length back and through, as well as in tempo, throughout the entire stroke.

To practice putting, take one ball, just as you would do on the course, and putt around the putting clock on the practice putting green. You'll notice the flags or metal cup markers are often numbered so that you can progress from one to another in sequence. You never have consecutive putts of the same lengths. This will help you develop your "feel" so that you can correlate the size of the stroke with certain distances, as well as variations caused through slopes, uphill, and downhill.

The back of the left hand should be toward the target to keep the putt on-line.

Putting Progression

A great distance control practice drill involves placing balls in a line at three-foot intervals moving away from the hole. Starting with the ball that is closest to the hole and moving back progressively to each ball, you should feel that the only variable is the length of the stroke back and through. You should not attempt to "hit" the longer putts harder but continue to stroke the ball at a

The distance-control practice drill called putting progression.

consistent tempo, allowing only the increase in the size of the stroke to increase the distance the ball will roll. Use this distance control drill on uphill, downhill, and sidehill putts as well.

Use Your Feet to Regulate the Size of Your Stroke

One common fault of beginner golfers is having very little feel for how large a putting stroke to make as the distance of putts change. So many of my beginning students lack this. This system, I have found, has made a huge difference for many of my students. The results I have seen were dramatic and quick. You must understand that this is not even close to being exact, but merely a place to start from. It was developed in an effort to avoid the embarrassment of being only 10 feet away from the hole, stroking your putt, and ending up 30 feet away, better known as the "hand explosion" putt. We have all experienced this. It is a bad thing when you hear someone say, "You're still away." I remember four-putting in a tournament in South Africa. My friend Kathy and I laughed when I told her the story, she more than I. I also told her at which hole my accident had occurred. She then proceeded to four-putt the same green the next day. The power of suggestion is very strong!

Assuming that your width of stance is somewhere around hip width, you can use your feet to regulate the size of your strokes. This will help you with your distance control.

Small putt: big toe to big toe.

Medium putt: little toe to little toe.

Large putt: two or three inches outside your right foot to two or three inches outside your left foot.

Extra large putt: five or six inches outside your right foot to five or six inches outside your left foot.

You will notice that no distances have been assigned to small, medium, large, and extra large. This is done on purpose. Greens vary in speed as well as uphill and downhill. Distance is something you will want to determine based on the greens that you are playing. It is amazing to me how my newest student and I will often label a putt exactly the same, small, medium, large, or extra large. I may have a putt I consider medium in length that is downhill; therefore, I will play it as a small putt. I may have a medium putt in length that is uphill; therefore, I will play it as a large putt.

Once again, this is merely a place for you to get started. I have seen tremendous success using this system. If you practice always verbally naming your putt to start and assigning a stroke size to that distance, I believe you will avoid those so embarrassing hand explosion putts.

Reading Greens

Very soon, as you practice putting, you will observe that many putts will break or fall off-line due to the slope of the green. The first step in attempting to read the line of your putt is looking at the bigger picture. Look at the overall slope on which the course is located. At the Broadmoor in Colorado, the course slopes away from the mountains. At Pebble Beach in California, the course slopes toward the ocean. This does not mean every putt at the Broadmoor will break away from the mountains or that every putt at Pebble will break toward the Pacific. Putts will just break more in that direction than you can see looking at the limited distance involved with your individual putt. Also, evaluate the slope of the individual green. Usually, one side of the green will be higher than the other, which is relatively easy to detect. Putts will tend to break toward the low side of the green. To test your green-reading skills, evaluate the overall slope of the green, then make a putt of about 10 to 15 feet to verify your read. The art and science of reading greens is very complex. Downhill putts will break more than the slope you see; uphill putts will break less. Putts will also occasionally have double, triple, and quadruple breaks; for example, a putt may break right in the first segment of a putt, go straight in the middle, and then break abruptly left in the last third of the putt. Then there is the matter of grain (the direction in which the grass grows), but this is a beginner's golf book. Grass blades will grow in the direction of the setting sun. Trying to deal with grain is definitely overkill for a beginner. Allow for the obvious and predominant break and leave the grain to the pros. You can, however, learn to plumb bob without acquiring paralysis by analysis.

A Little Trick

A little trick that I use in my own play, which we also teach at the Academy of Golf at PGA National under the direction of Mike Adams, is aiming short of the hole on downhill putts and aiming past the hole on uphill putts. Your eyes are not great at registering the undulations; they tend to pick up more of the distance. But this tricks your eyes into registering the downhill or the uphill. By aiming short of the cup on your downhill putts you can trick your eyes into believing that you have a shorter putt. By aiming past the cup on an uphill putt you can trick your eyes into believing that you have a longer putt. In both cases it is easier to putt the ball closer to the hole, because you have recognized both the distance and how the hill will affect the rolling of the ball.

Plumb Bobbing

You've seen the pros do it on telecasts: go through this strange ritual of dangling their putters in front of them, squinting at them as though they are about to deliver a message revealing mysteries. And they are! They are using the plumb bob method of reading the green or determining the break of slopes in the green. Yes, any beginning golfer can learn to plumb. But first, you must determine your master eye, because the putter must be sighted with your master eye.

First, select an object in the distance—a flagstick, a tree, a telephone, a fence post. Hold up a circle formed between your index finger and your thumb and align the object in the opening of the circle. Do not expect to be able to create sharp focus; you won't.

Now close your left eye and view the object combination with your left eye closed. If the object remains in the circle, you are right-eye dominant. But to be sure, close your right eye. The object should move outside the circle between your index finger and thumb.

Plumb bobbing.

Stand behind the ball, with the ball between yourself and the hole. With both eyes open turn your putter into a plumb line and hold the club loosely between your thumb and forefinger, the toe of the putter pointing either directly toward the hole or directly away from it. Let the shaft of the putter hang through the center of the hole. The shaft has now become the string on a plumb bob. Close your nondominant eye and now see that the shaft of the putter hangs to the left or to the right of the cup. You have now completed your read of the green by plumb bobbing. If the shaft aligns to the left of the cup, that is where you should align your putt, because it will then break to the right, and vice versa if the shaft aligns to the right of the cup.

Plumb bobbing is most helpful when you are in doubt about whether the putt breaks right or left.

My father taught me to plumb bob at a very young age. It is such a part of my putting routine today that I often do it without even thinking. I believe it helps me the most on unfamiliar courses, as well as putts I just am having a hard time reading.

Try to observe the green while you are waiting for your playing partners to putt. Is it uphill? Is it downhill? An uphill putt will break less than your read. A downhill will break more because the ball is rolling slower and thus is more susceptible to gravity.

Practice reading putts on the practice green and check your results. If you read a right break, did it actually break right? Reading greens accurately is a result of years of practice, and even then you will hear a television commentator say the player "misread it."

Lesson 11

How Do I Get This Little Ball into the Air?

It is crucial that your concept of how the golf ball gets into the air is very strong. This will help you to make the proper motion. The bottom of the club *must* get down to the ground to get the ball into the air. The ball must be contacted below its equator for it to get up into the air at all.

This is the opposite of what all tennis players are doing, or players of any racket sport for that matter. In tennis we swing up to make the ball go up, because the tennis racket has no loft. In golf the loft is built into the club head, so we must get the club down to the ground to get the ball into the air. Have you ever watched golf on TV, where you see the professionals taking out a big patch of turf? This is called a divot. A divot normally occurs on iron shots. When a divot is made it is made on the target side of the ball. The contact is made first with the ball and then the turf. It is amazing how many good players do not know this. So when the club contacts the golf ball, it is still on a downward path, progressing from the ball to even lower, then into the ground. We do *not* swing up to make the ball go up, as in many other sports. The club is on the downward path of the circle when it contacts the ground. It is not necessary that you take a divot with every iron shot, but you do need to understand that at the very least the club should stay very low to the ground in front of the ball. Low enough that if you were to place a tee in front of the ball, teed very low, the club head should contact the ball, the ball travel into the air, and then the club head progress low enough to also knock the tee in the ground in front of the ball out as well.

The bottom of the club must hit the ground for the golf ball to get into the air.

So, now you understand what should happen. Now we move on to the fact that many women do not like to hit the ground, a condition called terraphobia. This is definitely a female issue. Whether it is the fear that hitting the ground will hurt or the fear that they will make a mess, I have seen a consistent reaction among my female students the first time they actually hit the ground with their club. First, the apology— unnecessary, I might add. This is then followed by the immediate attempt to repair the damage. This repair is not necessary until after you are finished hitting your shot on the golf course or finished with your practice session on the range. Watch the men; they seem not to be worried about this. Terraphobia is a fear that must be over come. It should not hurt if you hit the ground. If it does, try to relax your arms more, so they do not absorb all of the shock. Place a tee or a small coin on the ground in front of the golf ball and practice hitting the ground enough to get the ball and the tee or coin into the air. One young lady I was teaching was definitely afraid to hit the ground. We took a bottle of divot mix from off the golf cart and made little piles of sand on the ground and placed a ball on top of the little pile. Divot mix is sand and seed mix that is placed on the golf carts or on the teeing area of the par 3s so that you can fill in your divot that you made. She then learned to hit the sand and the ball would travel into the air. This intermediate step allowed her to do very well from the ground. Also, realize it is OK to make a mess. Just look around you. There are probably divot holes all over the place. This is a very acceptable mess.

When practicing on the range, take a practice swing for each ball that you hit off the ground. Practice hitting the ground on the practice swing and repeat that feeling with the ball in the way. Once you overcome the fear of hitting the ground or making a mess the number of golf balls that travel into the air will, fortunately, increase.

Lesson 12
The Short Game— Chipping and Pitching

LESSON GLOSSARY

Bump and run: Also called pitch and run, a shot hit short of the pin, which then runs that balance of the distance to the cup.

Chip: A shot hit with a low-lofted club from close to the edge of the green, the majority of its length consisting of run along the ground, usually on the putting surface.

Flop shot: A shot hit with a sand wedge, which consists of almost all carry, or flight in the air, and very little roll.

Pitch: A shot hit with a high-lofted club, such as a sand wedge, the majority of its length consisting of carry.

Run-up: A shot hit with a very low-lofted club, from a 9 iron through a 5 iron. The majority of its length will consist of roll along the ground. This shot is used when circumstances are such that it would be unnecessarily risky to hit a pitch shot on the green. Typically a run-up is played close to a green when the pin is in the back of the green and you have a lot of short grass to cover. A run-up can be hit with a "Texas wedge," otherwise known as a putter. The chances for catastrophic error are greatly reduced by using a Texas wedge.

Approach Shots

An approach shot is one that is hit when the position of your ball on the course is so close to the green (putting surface) that a full swing with the shortest club in your set would cause you to go over the green. Obviously, an adjustment must be made. The most commonly made adjustment is a shortening of the backswing, thus limiting the velocity that can be attained on the downswing. Lowered velocity translates into lesser distance. You will learn after considerable and continuing practice how much backswing you need to hit a given distance, although don't expect to be able to announce, "Now I'm going to take a 34-inch backswing to hit a 28-yard pitch shot." It won't be like that. It will be more like tossing a ball underhand a specific distance—you feel the distance you must take your arm back; you do not measure the distance.

If you watch any amount of golf on television you will hear reference to a vareity of approach shots: chip, bump and run, pitch, cut, flop shot, lob wedge, explosion (from sand), run-up, and pitch and run. Without exception, all of these terms describe the amount of carry (flight in the air) in proportion to the amount of roll.

By now you are aghast at the complexity of the game. "I'll never learn all of those shots," you protest.

"Relax," I advise. "You don't have to learn all of those shots. You need to learn a chip, and you need to learn a pitch. All of the other shots are merely variations on those themes. You should never try to play a shot on the course that you have not practiced. Practicing all of those shots adequately to be able to play them on the course would require an investment in practice time you probably would be unwilling to make and should not be expected to make. In an effort to keep your initial learning experience as simple as possible, learn the basic motion, and you can learn to get fancy later. There are a lot of fancy ways to alter setup, which you can graduate to once you learn this basic motion. This will work very well in getting you started.

Chipping

Less Air Time, More Ground Time

You will chip from around the edges of the green when the distance from your golf ball to the edge of the green is smaller than the distance between the edge of the green and the pin. So, in other words, you will chip when you require less air time and more ground time.

The advantage to chipping is that you are taking a smaller swing, because much of the distance in which the ball travels is roll. The smaller the swing you take, the less chance of error.

Chipping is a shot that most of my students seem to enjoy. It is very low on the embarrassment scale. Whether I hit the chip perfectly and it travels into the air, landing just over the collar and onto the green, rolling the rest of the way to the pin, or I hit the ball incorrectly and do not get the club down to the grass, the shots do not end up looking that different. Oftentimes when you miss a chip, your playing partners cannot even tell that you did not hit the ball properly. We all like this.

I recommend that as a new player you choose a limited number of clubs with which you will chip. A pitching wedge (10 iron) and a 7 iron, for example. It is easier to adjust your swing size with two clubs, rather than confusing the issue by using all of your clubs. If you are in a situation where you require more roll than carry, use your pitching wedge (10 iron). If you are in a situation where you require a *lot* more roll than carry—for example, the pin way in the back of an uphill green—use your 7 iron. As the amount of roll you want increases, use the 7 iron rather than the pitching wedge, because the percentage of roll will be greater with a lesser lofted, relative to a pitching wedge, which will roll less.

Grip Down and Step in Closer

When setting yourself up to chip, you will want to grip down to the bottom of the grip and step in toward the golf ball. You can use either your full-swing grip or your putting grip. I have seen it done both ways successfully. If you use your putting grip, this can help you to keep your wrists from breaking down. This is the way we teach chipping at the Academy of Golf at PGA National, but I have always chipped with my normal full-swing grip—and not too badly, in my opinion. We look to be very accurate with both distance and direction. The lower I place my hands on the club and closer I step to the ball, the more in control I am. You will want your stance to be more narrow for chipping than for your full swing. There will be minimal amount of lower body motion. You can help to eliminate this motion by narrowing your feet.

When chipping, grip down and step in for more control.

Ball Back in Stance

Right for Roll

Place the ball in the back in your stance or more in line with the big toe of your right foot. The farther back into your stance you

For chipping, play the ball back in your stance in-line with the inside of your right foot. Remember, right for roll. Notice the shaft angles left toward the target.

play the ball, the more roll you will receive. With a chip in a rolling shot I find that many of my students forget where to position the golf ball within their stance, so simply remember "right for roll." These little ways to remember seem to really help. When you travel out to the golf course, these little rhymes are easier to utilize than the rote memorization.

Shaft Angles Left

When you allow your arms to hang naturally to the center of your body, the shaft of the club will angle toward the target so that the end of the grip of the club is in line with your left pocket. The end of the grip should hide behind your left arm.

This will slightly de-loft (take loft away) from the club face and produce a lower running shot. Be very careful that the club face continues to aim toward the target when you lean the handle forward, and that it does not twist open when aiming to the right.

Maintain the Triangle

There will be little or no wrist hinge in this shot. It should be a one-lever shot, as in putting. When you take your initial setup position, the grip end of your club will hang behind your left arm. It should maintain this relationship throughout the stroke. If you use your wrists excessively, the end of the club will change its position in relationship to your arms. The triangle formed by your arms and across your shoulder should continue to exist throughout your motion.

Weight Favors the Left

Your weight should favor your left foot throughout the stroke. This will help to eliminate unnecessary lower body motion, helping you to be more accurate with both distance and direction.

Also, when I place my weight onto my left foot this will drop my left shoulder slightly lower, which will help to produce a descending blow. The club head is on the downward path to the ground when it sweeps the grass, lofting the golf ball up and over the apron.

Notice the end of the grip of the golf club maintains its position behind the left arm when you maintain the triangle.

Sweep the Grass

Now concentrate on sweeping the grass. We have a saying in golf: "Let the club head do the work." This does not mean a club will hit the ball unaided. It means that the loft of the club will lift the ball into the air for you; you do not need to "help it up" by scooping with your right hand. It is necessary for the club to reach the ground to get the ball into the air. If we try to swing up as we would in tennis, for example, we contact the top of the ball with the bottom of the club, producing a "skull," which is a shot where the ball travels low, entirely across the ground, often traveling too far. Remember to assist the club in sweeping the grass; allow your weight to favor your left foot in your setup at the address position and throughout the stroke. This will help ensure a descending blow, which will produce an airborne shot.

Straight Back and Straight Through, As in Putting

The chip stroke should be straight back and straight through, as in putting. Use the railroad track system that you used in putting to practice this path, although allow more room between the club shafts.

The Quarter Drill

Place a quarter or any other coin on the ground on the target side of the golf ball. Make your chipping motion. If your golf club is sweeping the grass correctly, the coin as well as the golf ball should be airborne. The club head must stay low to the ground in front of the golf ball in order to accomplish this task.

Left: Notice both the ball and the coin in the air.

Right: Swing straight back and straight through, like putting. The club on the ground helps me to see the target line.

Above: The club head should stay low enough to the ground in front of the golf ball to sweep the grass so that a coin placed in front of the ball should travel into the air.

Summary

You can accomplish all of these setup requirements with a simple setup routine: Feet together, step left.

I found that many of my students were having a very hard time remembering all of these setup adjustments for chipping. So I developed a routine that would accomplish all of the necessary points with two little steps. It is so much easier. This routine will put you into a perfect position very quickly and efficiently, which requires less thought.

First, start with your feet right together, the ball in line with the center of your feet. Go ahead and grip down on the grip and step in closer for control. Aim your club face to your target at this point. Look up at your target.

Second, while still looking at your target, take your left foot and step it slightly left of your target. When you step left toward the target, allow everything to go with you. Allow the shaft of the club to angle left toward the target, so that the grip of the club is in line with your left pocket, and allow your weight to go left.

This setup routine has put the ball in perfect position, in line with your right foot. It has placed the weight to the left and has angled the shaft to the left, all with one little step to the left.

I have seen fantastic success from my students with this routine. The setup will automatically be perfect with one little step. Learn the routine, and then stick with the routine. It really works, and I hope it will help you. So remember, feet together, step left for chipping.

To summarize:

1. Less air time, more ground time.

2. Grip down and step in closer.

3. Ball back in stance.

4. Maintain the triangle.

5. Weight favors the left.

6. Sweep the grass.

7. **Straight back and straight through, as in putting.**

With the smaller swing required in the chip shot there is a greater margin for error. That is, a small mistake in a short swing does not translate into as big a shot-making error as the same mistake would in a longer swing. So the moral of the story is that it is preferable to chip, rather than pitch, because the chip shot is more forgiving, as long as your situation at hand dictates more roll than carry. Chip if you can; pitch if you have to.

To My Atlantic Ladies

Many of the ladies who I have the privilege to teach at Atlantic Golf Club love to bump and run (chip) the ball. If they could, they would bump and run every shot, even through the bunkers. They are correct in wanting to do this, because a bump and run is more forgiving than a pitch shot. The smaller swing provides more distance, therefore a smaller chance of error. You must, however, learn to pitch the ball for those situations where you have to go up and over.

Chipping Homework

1. Practice your feet together, step left routine to position yourself properly at address 10–15 times each day, until the weight moves left and the shaft angles left naturally as you make the step just left of your target.

2. Practice maintaining the triangle formed by your arms as the end of the grip of the club maintains its position behind your left arm.

3. Practice keeping your weight on your left foot so that the club is allowed to sweep the carpet in your house.

Pitching

If the distance between your golf ball and the edge of the green is greater than the distance between the edge of the green and the pin, you will pitch. Then you will have more air time in comparison to ground time, more carry than roll.

You will pitch the ball any time you need more carry than roll up to the distance that you can hit the sand wedge up to a full swing, from approximately 7 yards up to 40 to 50 yards.

Pitching is a pretty shot, because the ball will travel nice and high and land relatively softly. It is, however, a little less forgiving than chipping, so you will want to spend time practicing the motion.

Use Your Sand Wedge

You will use your sand wedge to pitch. Remember, "sand wedge" is just a confusing name for your 11 iron, so it will have a lot of loft in the club face. The increased loft in the club face will produce a shot that has a higher trajectory, producing more air time.

Position the Ball in the Center of Your Stance

You will want to position the golf ball in the center of your stance. This will produce pitch shots with the trajectory of the actual loft of the sand wedge—relatively high.

As you become a more experienced golfer, you can change your ball position to control trajectory to learn to hit the ball higher and lower. But let's stick to the basic motion for now.

Shaft Straight Up and Down

When you set up to pitch the golf ball, you want to leave the shaft of the club straight up and down so that the end of the grip

When pitching the ball, play the ball in the center of your stance and notice how the end of the club (the tee also) points to your belly button.

points toward your belly button. Do not lean the shaft to the left toward the target as you did in chipping. If you inappropriately lean the shaft to the left, this will take loft away from the club and produce a lower and running shot, which is not what you are looking for in this situation.

Short Pitches

Your short pitches will be a smaller motion of just arm swing. Your short pitches are from approximately 6 to 20 yards. Your body motion will be minimal.

You will want to place your hands lower onto the grip of the club and to narrow your stance. This will give you more control. At the Academy of Golf, Mike Adams uses the setup to control the size of the swing. He calls it "dial a wedge." This system really works. I have adopted a smaller version of this system.

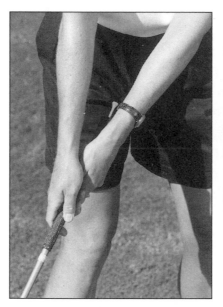

For your small pitches, notice that the tee in the end of the grip maintains its position between your forearms in your backswing.

And your forward swing.

Your arms should be relaxed and hanging. Your wrist hinge will be minimal. Not because you are tight, but because with this small of a swing, your wrists do not naturally activate. Note that the tee in the end of the grip of the club maintains its position throughout the arm swing.

Set your golf club onto the ground and assume your golf posture. Practice the motion of just swinging your arms and notice that when you are totally relaxed your wrists do not move excessively for this motion.

The size of this swing should be approximately knee level to knee level.

Medium Pitches

Your medium pitches will travel approximately 15 to 30 yards. I am not able to tell you an exact distance due to the fact that we all hit the ball different lengths based upon our strength as well as the quality of our technique. So, practice each of these pitches: small, medium, and large, and see how far *you* hit each.

When you set up to hit a medium pitch you will still want to grip down on the handle of the club, but not quite as much as for the small pitch, approximately to the center of the grip. You will also want to narrow your stance, but not as much as for the small pitch.

For your medium pitch you will allow your club to swing back and through to about hip level. Your wrist hinge will be slight to minimal. In a swing of hip level and below, your wrists will not naturally activate. Due to the fact that you are making a larger swing (hip to hip) your body will start to become more active. Allow what your body wants to happen to happen naturally. As

Percentage backswings control your distance in your pitch shots. A half swing for medium sized pitches.

your club swings toward the target your right heel should naturally start to come off of the ground, as it would if you were to throw a ball underhand at this distance.

Large Pitches

Your large pitches will travel approximately 40 to 50 yards in distance. You will want to grip the handle of the club toward the top of the grip, at the club's full length, and you will want to widen your stance to hip width.

As you move farther away from your target, it will be necessary for you to increase the length of your backswing, and therefore you must allow your right arm to fold on the backswing, which is naturally accompanied by a wrist hinge. In addition, you should allow your left arm to fold on your forward swing. Your larger pitches will look like percentage golf swings. They start to take on more of a full swinging motion. The greater the distance you need the ball to carry, the larger the swing you will make. As the swing increases in size, so does the amount of body motion. Your small chips and pitches will have very little body motion and be mostly arm swing. As you progress to medium-length pitches, your body motion will increase proportionally up to large pitches, where the body is allowed full natural motion.

A three quarter back swing for larger pitches.

You Do Have Distance Control

New golfers often feel as if they have no distance control whatsoever. This is totally false. You have a lot more control than you even know. If you know how far you hit a club in a full swing, with a little fifth-grade math you can see you, too, have distance control.

If in a full swing I hit my sand wedge 60 yards, how much of a swing do I need to carry the ball 30 yards? Well 30 equals one-half of 60, so I need a half-swing, which is where the club swings approximately hip-high to hip-high. Sounds easy, huh? It is! If I hit my pitching wedge 70 yards and I want to carry the ball 25 yards, as 25 is approximately one-third of 70, I need one-third of my swing, which is a swing where the club travels back just below hip level on your right side, through to just below hip level on your left side. This requires you to have a grasp on the length you hit each club, or just take the time to come up with a handy-dandy yardage chart as discussed earlier. Practice this and you will be amazed the distance control you do have, even as a beginner.

My brand-new golfers are amazed when they see that they do have distance control. It is much easier to not take responsibility for being able to control distance. But take the time to first figure out how far in yards it is to your target. You will then want to decide what club you will be hitting. Figure out what percentage of that club's full distance you will need for the appropriate shot. When you take your practice swing, be sure to make the exact size swing you will need for the shot. Remember that if it is a small shot, you will grip down and narrow your stance to help to limit the length of your swing.

Pitching Homework

Place a tee in the end of the grip of your club and practice at home keeping the tee centered in your forearms as you would for smaller pitches, which are just arm swing. This will help limit wrist hinge in an effort to scoop or lift the ball inappropriately and give you more control, and more forgiving shots, due to fewer moving parts to get you into trouble. Try to accomplish this

10 times a night for 10 days in a row. Practice sweeping your carpet with your small pitching motion. This will help you learn to get the club down to the ground and the golf ball to travel into the air.

The Importance of the Short Game

The short game is crucial. There is often a feeling of needing to learn the full swing first, because you need to be able to get around the edges of the green before you need to know how to chip and pitch. I understand this feeling. But keep in mind that the short game will help you with your full swing. The motion of pitching is the motion of your full swing, so as you are working on small, medium, and large pitches you are working on a smaller version of your full swing.

This past season I spent a lot of time teaching pitching in the golf school at PGA National. I really enjoyed working in this area, because as pitching utilizes a percentage of the full swing we were able to identify students' full-swing flaws before they even arrived in their full-swing rotation. By the time they rotated from pitching to full swing they had already addressed a lot of the issues they needed to work on in their full swing. Also, with a few key checkpoints pitching is not difficult at all. We were able to help these students to become very successful pitchers of the golf ball, and it is always fun to see progress for the student as well as the instructor.

Instructor Versus Students

My friend Jeff Warne, whom I have the privilege to teach with at the Atlantic Golf Club in Bridgehampton, New York, in the summer and who also teaches at Doral for Jim McLean, has a little competition with his students to show them the importance of the short game. During a lesson he will have the student play his or her own ball up to the point where he or she has an approach shot into the green. Jeff will then drop a golf ball next to the student's golf ball and play his ball into the hole, and the student continues to play his or her own ball into the hole. They then compare their scores. This will illustrate to the student the importance of the short game. The students are amazed at the difference in scores between Jeff's short game and their own. This is good motivation to practice.

Lesson 13
The Full Swing

The full swing is the technique most often used on the golf course, since it is the technique that will yield the greatest distance from given clubs. A full swing is nothing more, nothing less, than an elongated pitch shot. You will find that your small and medium pitch shots will be the bottom half of your full swing. A full swing is probably most distinguished from approach shots in the length of the swing and the fact that the wrists are fully hinged. The body is also complete in its rotation.

Underhand Throwing Motion

The motion of the golf swing is that of an underhand throwing motion. Most all of us have thrown a ball at one point in our lives. By practicing this motion you will feel the natural motion of the body that you will want in your full swing. If you are new to golf, I recommend that you actually practice throwing golf balls to feel how the body should work.

I was practicing this with one of my students back when I first started teaching golf about 10 years ago. It was very obvious to me, after my student's first attempt, that she had never played baseball. She made a reasonably good underhand motion, but she then forgot to let go of the golf ball until very late, so that it ended up going over our heads, landing on the cart path behind of us. So I had her try to throw the ball again. Once again she forgot to let go. We caused quite a scene, but we stuck with the throwing motion until she could throw the ball properly. You have to laugh at yourself in situations like this. Some areas of golf will come to you very easily, and some will take more perseverance. If you persevere, you will accomplish your goals.

Do Not Be Afraid to Miss the Golf Ball

When you are working on your golf swing or any other motion in golf, you need to be willing enough to try new things. When you make a new and different motion, you run a chance of totally missing the golf ball. This is fine at this point. Avoid being so concerned with missing the ball that you are not willing to make the appropriate swing improvements. It is OK to miss the ball at this point.

When I was learning to play golf, I played it with my father almost every day. When I got upset because I missed a shot my father would say to me, "You've done that before and you are going to do it again." He was and continues to be correct. This is the reality of golf.

Solid Fundamentals

When you start to work on your full swing, your pre-swing fundamentals must be good. Your grip and your setup must be correct.

These fundamentals will absolutely affect your ability to swing the club properly.

I attended a teaching seminar at Bay Hill in Orlando with the well-known golf instructors Jim McLean, Craig Harmon, Butch Harmon, and Mike McGetrick. They spent three days stressing how important these fundamentals are to the golf swing. They also explained that the setup fundamentals are the most common areas that they are working on with their golf swings. I recently had the privilege of watching Jim McLean work with a senior tour player, at the Doral Resort and Spa in Miami, Florida and all they worked on was the setup.

If your golf professional wants you to work on your grip and you are not thrilled because the change is not comfortable, just remember that you will not be able to make the proper swing without the proper grip.

The Golf Swing Is a Very Simple Motion

We often make the golf swing more complicated than it is in reality. I have included seven points that I feel are important to the motion of the golf swing. But keeping the motion very simple is very important. When we teach our ladies in our Women Teaching Women program at PGA National we see fantastic successes through keeping the motion very simple.

Take the correct grip and setup. Tee up a golf ball. Place a tee approximately two feet straight in front of the ball and two feet straight behind the ball. Both of these tees should be on the target line. Swing the club head, staying relatively low to the ground for several inches to start straight back over the tee behind the golf ball. The club head should swing back on a line that is parallel to your toe line. Your left under arm should stay connected to your chest. As you swing the club back along this line, with the left arm connected, the connection will naturally pull your body to turn. Once you complete your backswing, you should simply make an underhand throwing motion toward the target, allowing the body to naturally follow the club swinging toward the target. Keep in mind that the rotation of the body will happen naturally; it should not have to be forced. Read through the seven cardinal points of the full swing to understand, but keep the motion as simple as you possibly can.

The Seven Cardinal Points of the Full Swing

1. Centered Rotation About the Spine

The torso should rotate around the spine. The shoulders should turn away from the target on the backswing and toward the target on the forward swing and turn 90 degrees on the backswing and

For your full swing, you should be centered and rotary in your backswing.

And your forward swing.

180 degrees from that position to face the target on the forward swing. The shoulders should neither dip nor tilt. To practice this, cross your arms across your chest, bending forward from your hips, as in your normal golf setup, and practice turning back and forth.

On your back turn, your right knee should maintain its flex if you are turning properly. On your forward, turn toward the target and as your torso turns forward your right knee should move around to come close to your left knee. Your belt buckle and hips should face the target. Your right foot should turn up to the toe, so that a person behind you looking down the target line should see the bottom or the spikes of your right shoe.

The left underarm stays connected to the body, which promotes the proper rotation.

2. Connection

The left under arm is connected to the body throughout your rotation. This will allow your club to travel on a proper path as well as to help coordinate the timing of the arms and the body so that they work together. Your connection to your body will also pull your torso to rotate naturally, so it is something that happens rather than something you need to overthink. It is also much easier to generate power if your arms are connected to your body, rather than separate and working independently. Keep in mind this is only the upper part of the arm, the under arm not the elbow, because that will cause you to lose width in your swing. You can practice this by keeping a head cover under your left arm and taking some practice swings. If you are staying connected properly, the head cover should not fall out from underneath your arm. Jimmy Ballard, whom I had the privilege to watch teach at Doral, was a huge advocate of connection. I have found connection to be a very important part of my golf swing. I played some of my most successful golf on the ladies' Asian Tour by simply working on staying connected.

3. Width

The radius of your circle will be wide! The club head should stay wide away from you during the circle of the swing. A fully extended circle will be a maximum width you can repeat. If you were to vary your width, this would produce inconsistency. Width means

The left arm travels approximately at ten o'clock in the backswing. Also notice that my weight has naturally transferred to my right foot as my upper body turns around my spine.

The left arm connection allows me to keep the head cover in its position under my left arm. Also note the width of the forward swing.

stretching on your backswing; it does not mean swinging the club away from your body so that your left underarm does not stay against your chest. The width or stretch is very important, because it will help to minimize your topped shots, where the club does not get down to the ground to get the golf ball into the air. Keeping the width of the backswing the length of the backswing, the left arm should travel to somewhere between 9 o'clock and 10 o'clock, dependent upon your flexibility, but no farther.

Practice working on the width and the length of your backswing in a mirror. Feel the stretch. Your arms should not collapse in toward your body. When you complete the length of your backswing your left arm should not swing past approximately 10 o'clock and your hands should finish to the right side of your head. They should never collapse so that your hands hide behind your head.

On your wide forward swing, your club head should swing out to your target until your arms naturally fold to finish around you.

4. Weight Transfer

On your backswing rotation, your weight should transfer onto a flat right foot, with your right knee maintaining its initial flex.

On your forward swing rotation, your weight should transfer over to a flat left foot.

This should happen relatively naturally. As the golf club swings, your weight should naturally transfer to follow the direction of the club.

This lateral motion will not be excessive. The weight transfer occurs as the body turns

The weight should transfer to the left foot on the forward swing. The foot has been lifted only to point out that the weight has fully transferred, and should not happen in reality.

to the right of the spine on the backswing, causing the weight to transfer, and as the body turns to the left of the spine on the forward swing, causing the weight to transfer.

5. Feeling and Swinging the Club Head

Almost all of the weight of the golf club is in the club head. The club head should swing freely throughout the golf swing. The club head swinging will cause your wrists to hinge on the backswing and unhinge on the forward swing in reaction to your body motion. This will require you to be somewhat relaxed to be able to properly feel the weight in the club head.

If I start to feel myself getting too tight or holding onto the club too tightly, I will take several practice swings trying to relax enough to start to feel the club head swing naturally. When I try to overcontrol the club head through tension I never hit the ball as well as when I stay relaxed.

To acquire the feeling of the club head swinging, stand with your feet together. Feel that the club is very heavy on the end. If you cannot feel that heaviness, grip the club head end of the club on the shaft below the club head and swing it for contrast. Then return the club to its normal position and you should be able to feel the difference. In both scenarios the grip of the club when it is held upside down and the head of the club when it is held properly should make a "swooshing" noise on the forward swing.

No matter how short or how far you hit the golf ball, you will want to be able to hit it farther. It is just human nature. Those that hit it straight want to hit it far, and visa versa. It will be necessary for you to develop some fundamentals to be able to hit the ball with some consistency. It is necessary to hit the ball in the clubface to get any distance at all. So your first goal is to develop a swing that has solid fundamentals, and then you can work on increasing the distance you are able to hit the ball.

In your effort to hit the ball far you must understand that it is the speed you can generate with your club head that gives you distance. The more *swoosh* you can make the farther the ball will travel. There is a great difference between faster and harder. Faster is good and harder is not. If I try to swing the club harder I will induce tension and lose speed. Practice swooshing the grip end of your club and the club head side. You will feel a big difference in the weight of the club head versus the grip end. Teach yourself to swoosh the club and you will feel the difference between faster, which is good and harder which makes you lose distance.

If there is balance in your golf swing, you should be able to hold your finish until the ball lands. Notice full rotation on the forward swing has pulled the right foot all the way up to the toes.

6. Tempo

Tempo should be smooth and consistent enough to put the club into a good position, generate force, and maintain balance. The swing should accelerate so the club head makes that "swoosh" noise. There is a balance between tempo and swinging so hard that you fall off balance. We want to maintain balance but generate club head swing. Practice "swooshing" the grip of the club to learn the difference between swinging the club fast, which is good and will produce club head speed, and swinging the club hard, which is bad because it will often cause you to lose balance, as well as increase tension decreasing club head speed.

7. Balance

The golfer needs to stay in balance throughout the golf swing. The body should be in balance at the top of the backswing and at the finish position. A golfer with good finishing balance will tend to go through the contact zone more consistently, producing solid ball contact. If you find yourself falling off balance during your golf swing, check your setup, and then work very hard to hold your finish position. Try to get into the habit of holding your finish position until the ball lands on the ground from out of the air.

Check to see that your golf swing is in accordance with each of these seven points, but remember: try to keep motion as simple as possible.

Lesson 14
What'd I Do Wrong, Coach?

LESSON GLOSSARY

Topped shot: A shot in which the ball is contacted on its top with the bottom of the club, with the result that the ball rolls along the ground. Complete whiffs are in this category.

"Fat" shot: A shot in which the turf was struck before the ball or too much turf was struck in the swing. The result is a shot that goes a far shorter distance than the club is capable of hitting.

Shank: A shot hit in the heel or hosel of the neck of the club, with the result that the ball leaves the club at nearly a right angle and has a low flight.

Toed shot: A shot hit on the toe of the club. The result is that the ball flies severely to the right and often high as well. The shot will often leave a telltale ball mark on the toe of the club.

Skied shot: A shot hit with a wood where the ball travels very high in the air (a pop-up), often leaving a ball mark on the top of the club.

Push: A shot hit on the center of the club face, or close to it, that goes to the right, usually with a high trajectory, without a curve.

Slice: A shot that curves from left to right, caused by a clockwise spin on the ball.

Hook: A shot that curves from right to left, caused by a counter-clockwise spin on the ball.

Pull: A shot hit in the center of the club face, or close to it that goes to the left, without a curve.

Inside out: The path of the club, which travels from the player away from the player. This will not by itself cause a hook; an inside-out path must be accompanied by a closed club face relative to the path.

Outside in: A club path that travels away from the player toward the player. An outside-in path by itself will not cause a slice; an outside-in path must be accompanied by an open club face relative to the path.

Error Correction

By now in your golf career, you may have concluded that there are unlimited ways of hitting the ball badly, simply by combining your bad shots. So when your teaching professional asks you at your next lesson what your predominant shot-making error is, you don't have to respond with a puzzled look. Your capability to describe your most prevalent shot-making error guides your teaching professional to the most direct route to correcting your error. Shot-making errors can be divided into two major categories:

DIRECTIONAL ERRORS	ERRORS IN CONTACT
Hook	Shank
Slice	Topped ball
Push	"Fat" shot
Pull	Toed shot
	Skied shot

Directional Errors

Very few golfers will hit the ball absolutely straight, even the pros. So, if you develop a tendency to hit the ball consistently in the wrong direction, there's probably a simple cure for it. But before you can tell your pro about your complaint, you must identify it. Avoid, however, calling any shot that goes to the right a slice and any shot that goes to the left a hook. You may be just hitting pushes and pulls. The correction for those shots is very different from that for slices and hooks!

The path of the club through what we call the hitting area (roughly, 1 foot to 18 inches on either side of the ball) and the club face will determine the direction in which the ball travels. Slices and hooks are caused by combinations of the club path and the position of the club face at impact with the ball. Keep in mind here that the manner in which you put your hands on the club controls the club face squareness at impact.

Once an error has developed to a significant level of consistency (for example, for the last two rounds you have been topping the ball consistently) and before you allow it to become a habit, make an appointment for a golf lesson and tell your pro what has been going on so he or she can focus on the correction.

"I'll have a student come in for a lesson," recalls a busy teaching professional, "and I'll say to her, 'And how long has this been going on?' I can predict the response. 'Oh, about six months,' the pupil will often say." That grooving an error before you start working on it makes it tough on the pro and the pupil. Nip an error in the bud. It is not going to go away by itself.

One of the reasons you take golf lessons is that you can't see yourself swing and, even if you could, you probably lack the golf background to correct your own errors. When you develop a consistent error, see your professional!

Keep in mind that there are numerous reasons for mishit shots. Included are some of the most common. Always refer back to your fundamentals, which include grip and setup.

Hook

This shot results from putting a counterclockwise spin on the ball, which sounds like it requires a great deal of talent and club head maneuvering, but if you hook you'll declare hooking is quite easy. I have had my fair share of hooks, which in my opinion are quite easy to do. You can ask my friend Kathy Hart Wood. When we played our practice rounds together in South Africa I would hook the ball and she would slice the ball. We would never see each other except on the putting green and the next tee.

Cause: **Too strong a grip (a grip in which one or both of your hands are rotated too far to the right). Too strong a grip places the hands in a position so they "roll over" rapidly on the downswing, closing the club face as they naturally seek the position in which the arms hang.**

Correction: **Place your hands on the club so that the Vs between your thumbs and forefingers point to your right shoulder, not your right hip.**

Cause: **Club face closed at address.**

Correction: **"Square up" the club face so the lower edge is at a right angle to the intended line.**

Cause: Arms outracing the body on the forward swing.

Correction: Keep the tempo of the arms and the body in sync during the swing. Feel as if there is a string between your belly button and the end of the grip of the club and try to keep this string in a line on the forward swing.

Cause: A closed stance at address, where your feet and body aim too far right of your target.

Correction: Square hips, feet and shoulders to be parallel to your target line.

Slice

A slice is a shot that I see the majority of women fighting. The main problem is that the ball travels a shorter distance due to the speed-reducing spin that is produced as a result of the club face being open. It is so much fun to watch students who had been slicing the ball when they start to hit the ball straight. As the ball travels so much farther it is great to see the looks on their faces. I spent this last winter working with one of my students, Susan. Our goal was to eliminate her slice and reverse the spin on the ball to produce a slight draw or even a hook. This was giving her more overspin and more distance. By the end of the winter she was missing the shots over the green. That was the kind of mistake we were looking for.

A slice curves excessively from left to right. The ball must be given a clockwise spinning action, which means it must be cut across with the club face open. Are you sure you slice?

Cause: Too weak a grip position. Either one hand or both are rotated too far to the left. Too weak a grip places the hands in a position where the club face opens on the forward swing as your arms seek the natural position they hang during the swing.

Correction: Place your hands on the club so that the Vs between your thumbs and forefingers point to your right shoulder, not your left shoulder.

Cause: Club face open at address.

Correction: "Square up" the club face so the lower edge is at a right angle to the intended line.

Cause: A shoulder tilt rather than a 90-degree shoulder turn on the backswing.

Correction: Practice turning your shoulders 90 degrees on the backswing so your shoulders rotate, rather than up and down. You can practice this by crossing your arms across your chest and working on turning the buttons on your shirt back away from your target.

Cause: The body outracing the arms on the forward swing.

Correction: Keep the tempo of the arms and the body in sync during the swing. Feel as if you have more arm swing on your forward swing, allowing your body to react to your arms.

Cause: An open stance at address, where your feet and body aim too far left of your target.

Correction: Square hips, feet, and shoulders to be parallel to your target line.

Push

A push is when the ball flies straight, but to the right of your target. The ball will usually travel the intended distance, but will end up to the right.

Cause: misalignment.

Correction: You may not actually be pushing the ball, just aiming too far to the right. Check that your club face aims to the target and that your feet and body are parallel to the target line.

Cause: Ball position too far to the right in your stance, which will also cause your shoulders to aim too far to the right.

Correction: Check your ball position: center for the irons and long irons; fairway woods, just left of center; and teed woods in-line with the instep of the left foot.

Cause: Club traveling too far behind your back on your backswing due to an early shoulder turn.

Correction: Allow your arms to swing back, parallel to your toes on your take-away.

Pull

A pull is when the ball flies straight, but to the left of your target. The ball will usually travel longer than your intended distance.

Cause: misalignment.

Correction: Check your alignment to see that the club face is aiming to the target and that your feet are parallel to the target and not left.

Cause: Ball position too far left of center, which would cause your shoulders to aim left.

Correction: Check your ball position: center for the irons; long irons and fairway woods, just left of the center; teed woods in-line with the instep of the left foot.

Cause: Incorrectly starting the down swing with the upper body and the shoulders, rather than the rotation of the torso.

Correction: Allow the hands and arms to be more passive in starting the down swing and allow the natural rotation of the body to pull them through. You may want to practice throwing a ball underhand to achieve this feeling.

Errors in Contact

Shank

A shank is definitely not a fun miss. In the resulting shot, not a pretty one, the ball often travels directly right and low.

Once the manager at Atlantic was out playing golf with the manager from another club on Long Island and since they were playing quicker than my foursome we waved them to play through. The visiting manager had a brutal case of the shanks. He just kept shanking the golf ball in a circle right around the green. Eventually he just picked up his golf ball. It was painful to watch him circle around the green, shanking the golf ball, ending up farther away from the pin after each shot.

Cause: The club head getting outside the ball, so that the ball is contacted in the neck or hosel of the club.

Correction: Obtain a head cover or a towel from off your golf bag. Lay it down about three or four inches away from your golf ball, on the side of the ball farther away from you and on your intended line of flight. Then swing the club without contacting the head cover or towel. If your club crosses outside the ball, the ball will probably hit the heel. Practice with the head cover or towel until you stop hitting the box, and your shanks should disappear. In my opinion, you do not want to place anything solid on the outside of the ball, if you shank the ball, you *do* get your club outside the ball. Place something soft, so that when you do make this incorrect motion you will be aware of your mistake, but you will not run the risk of injuring yourself. I have seen people practicing this with wooden boards. It does not seem worth the risk to me. So if this is your problem, please use something soft.

Cause: Not properly squaring the club face at impact, which will leave the face of the club open, exposing the hosel of the club to the ball.

Correction: Practice making half-swings. Hold your finish to check to see if the toe of your club is up or skyward, rather than having the face of the club skyward. If your club face is pointing to the sky so that you could serve a drink on your club face you have not allowed the club to naturally rotate through with your body.

Cause: Addressing the ball in the hosel at setup.

Correction: Address the ball in the center of the club face. It may appear more out toward the toe of the club from the player's perspective.

Cause: Left hand grip rotated too far to the left.

Correction: **Hold grip in fingers, so that the palm faces
toward your body and you can see two to three knuckles.**

Players who shank their shots will not like their irons. They will
tend to prefer the woods, simply because the woods do not have a
hosel and the irons do. You can spot shankers by their golf bags.
They will have a lot of woods, and their irons will have dimple
marks in the heels of the clubs. When they first start to understand the reason that they do not like their irons, because they are
contacting the ball in the hosel, they are on the road to being able
to correct the problem. You must first understand what you are
doing incorrectly, and then you must understand what you need
to change to make that correction.

Topped Ball

A topped ball, though very common, can be very frustrating to a
new golfer. You will hit some tops. It is just part of your initiation
process into the game of golf. Over time your percentage of tops
should decrease, but expect some of this in the first couple of
years. The suggestions here are to help you minimize your tops.

When I arrived at Furman University with approximately a 4
handicap, I would top my fairway woods once in a while. I was so
embarrassed I would wait to practice them when the range was
nearly empty. If a 4 handicap can top the ball, it is OK for you. I
forced myself to practice the fairway woods. Working on the
weak points of your game is not as much fun as practicing what
you are good at, but it will help you to improve.

I was giving a playing lesson when one of my students,
Carole, topped the golf ball off the tee of a par 3. I quickly picked
up the golf ball and placed it back onto her tee to try again. She
then proceeded to knock the golf ball into the hole. It was quite
an impressive par!

Cause: If you have a great deal of tension in your arms, this will cause the muscles in your arms to contract, which in turn causes your arms to pull in toward you.

Correction: Relax adequately so that you can feel the club head swinging freely.

Cause: Terraphobia, fear of hitting the ground.

Correction: Place a tee in the ground in front of your golf ball, and allow the club head to stay very low to the ground in front of the ball, which will allow you to use the loft of the club properly. Many women fear hitting the ground for two reasons: it will hurt or it will make a mess. It should not hurt unless you are "death-gripping" the club, and it is OK to make a mess, also known as a divot.

Cause: A lack of understanding of how the ball gets into the air.

Correction: Understand that the lower side of the club must be allowed to swing down to the ground to get the ball into the air. There is a phrase in golf "let the club head do the work." The true meaning is "permit the loft of the club to lift the ball into the air for you." Our tennis players must specifically watch this. In tennis you must swing up to get the ball into the air, because the tennis racket has no loft. In golf, we must get the club down to the ground to get the ball into the air. So in other words, we are hitting the ball as the club travels on a descending path.

Cause: Standing too far away from the golf ball.

Correction: Check your setup to make sure that there is only one hand's distance between the end of the grip of the club and your body.

Cause: Your weight is too much back toward your heels.

Correction: Bend forward from your hip joint, so that your chest is over your toes.

Cause: Loss of spine angle, also known as "standing up."

Correction: Maintain posture throughout the swing until contact with the ball.

"Fat" Shot

A fat shot occurs when you hit the ground before the golf ball. The ball will travel significantly shorter than anticipated.

Cause: Standing too close to the ball.

Correction: Back away from the ball adequately, so that you have approximately a hand's width, fingers outstretched, between the end of the golf club and your legs.

Cause: Tilting, rather than turning on your swing. If your shoulders dip, rather than turning around your spine, when your right shoulder drops on the forward swing the ground will often be contacted before the ball. Cross your arms across your chest and practice turning around your spine, so that your sternum turns away from the target, rather than the shoulders' teeter-tottering.

Cause: Staying too flat-footed on your forward swing.

Correction: As you make a natural underhand throwing motion on your forward swing you should allow your body to turn to face the target so that your right foot comes up to the toe in reaction to the body turning to face the target. The turning of the body toward the target will pull the club to swing through toward the target.

Toed Shot

This is a shot hit off the toe or tip of the club. It usually goes 90 degrees to the right and is potentially lethal. Do not allow anyone to stand directly to the right of you when you are practicing if you tend to toe your shots. Or place something like your golf bag to the right of the ball, to stop the ball from advancing too far to the right.

I was giving a lesson in New York right next to two other lessons. My student proceeded to toe the ball excessively off the end of the wood. The ball ever so softly lofted right over the instructor and the student directly to our right and landed like a marshmallow on the chest of the instructor two doors down. It landed so softly it was unbelievable. Nobody was hurt, but it was amazing to see the golf ball go so high, so right, and so short.

Cause: Standing too far away from the ball.

Correction: Determine if you have only one hand's distance (fingers extended) between the end of the club and your legs.

Cause: Arms pulling in on forward swing.

Correction: Work on swinging wide on the forward swing. Place a tee several inches ahead of your ball, along your flight line. Try to hit that tee as you swing through the ball. You will also want to check hand position in your grip. If your grip is too weak or, in other words, your hands rotated too far to the left, you will often try to pull across the ball to square the club face, causing you to pull in and toe the ball.

Cause: Loss of spine angle.

Correction: Maintain posture throughout the swing, as opposed to standing up. Your weight should maintain its position on the balls of your feet and not throw back to your heels at any point in the swing.

Skied Shot

A skied shot or a pop-up with your teed woods is a ball that travels excessively high and not very far.

Cause: Incorrect ball position.

Correction: Make sure that your ball position for your teed woods is left in your stance, in line with the inside of your left foot.

Cause: Too steep an angle of attack. The angle at which the club head comes into the golf ball is the angle at which the ball will come off the club head.

Correction: Feel that your swing is more circular, rather than resembling the letter **V**. Take practice swings where your club sweeps an extended patch of grass, rather than digging into the ground. You should not take a divot with a teed wood.

Bad advice that is often give to the beginner who is popping the golf ball up is to tee the ball lower. What you actually want to do is tee the ball higher. When the ball is teed too low, the student feels the necessity to go down to get the golf ball and dives, producing too steep an angle of approach. So tee the ball higher and practice not hitting the ground but sweeping the golf ball off the high tee. *Golf Digest Woman* published a great article on how a woman should interpret her husband's advice. This was one of the pieces of advice that they addressed. It was truly a great article, and this is a magazine I recommend, along with *Golf for Women*.

Keep a Notebook for Progress

We all tend to repeat our mistakes, so keep a small notebook of your problems with your golf and what you and your professional do to correct that particular problem. If that particular problem resurfaces, you can refer back to your notebook and correct your problems quicker. If we learn from our mistakes, they are worth making!

Lesson 15
Home on the Range

Ball machine: A machine designed to dispense practice or range balls. Wire baskets are normally used to contain the balls.

Ball machine tokens: Tokens especially designed to fit into the ball machines. Customers purchase tokens in the range office and then proceed to the ball machine. In exchange for a specified number of tokens, the machine dispenses range or practice balls into a wire basket.

Driving range: Public area, varying from a basic fairway and teeing grounds, usually consisting of artificial grass mats from which to hit, to a range with offices and sometimes a golf shop or pro shop from which merchandise is sold and usually with a practice putting green.

Golf learning center: An elaborate driving range, including short game practice areas and a section reserved for videotape analysis of students' swings or other high-tech analysis of swings.

You can often spot a new golfer at the driving range from a mile away, even before she starts to swing. Novices tend to look a little lost and a little nervous. The purpose of this chapter is to give you confidence in what is expected and how to handle yourself. This is to allow you to "fake it 'til you make it," which is one of my goals for each and every one of my new golfers.

Commercial practice facilities are available in every community. They vary from the unembellished, such as an old-fashioned driving range offering a few chopped-up teeing areas and a shack from which the dubious-quality range balls are dispensed to first-class golf learning centers, often offering a two-level teeing area, plus short-shot practice greens, putting courses (to be distinguished from kids' play miniature golf courses), elaborate golf schools, and clubhouses with golf shops and gourmet restaurants. Often these learning centers have three or more short golf holes associated with them, ideal for beginning play.

Facilities in your area are listed in the telephone book's yellow pages, usually under "Golf Driving Ranges." For your indoctrination on the range, go there and observe the activity.

Golfers drive into the parking lot, change their shoes in the car, retrieve their clubs from the trunk, and leave their golf bags on racks provided while they go into the shop. Most facilities do not want golf bags to be taken into the golf shop, as shoplifting clubs directly into the golf bags is thus made too easy. Either buy practice balls directly off the shelves or purchase tokens for the automatic ball dispensers now available at many driving ranges. Try not to forget to put a wire basket under the machine's dispenser as you put in your tokens. The result if you forget to put the basket under the dispenser will be a mess of balls everywhere. We have all done this, forgotten to put that stupid little basket under the dispenser. Learn from my mistake and remember the basket.

Try not to look like a neophyte as you carry your clubs. An experienced golfer will carry her clubs across her back, one hand resting on the clubs, which extend from the bag. When you are beginning your practice session, walk to the far left side of the range. Place your clubs in the rack, which is usually provided, and pour your practice balls out into the tray, beside the mat from which you will be hitting. The reason for practicing on the left side of the range is so that others will be facing away from you and will not, you hope, be paying you any attention. This is where I like to take all of my lessons. Most everyone is facing away from you except the occasional lefty. This is the least intimidating place to practice, because you can see most everyone, but they cannot see you because they are facing away from you.

Before you begin your practice session it is a good idea to do some stretching to warm up your muscles. Also, take some practice swings to continue to warm yourself up, stretch, and wake up those golf muscles. It is often a good idea to start your practice session with some short shots. Several chips and pitches will start you out positively, as well as warm you up and thus avoid injury. Starting with your short game makes a lot of sense. It helps to learn to walk before you try to run.

My student Jeanne always warms up with the half-swings. I encourage all my students to do this. This is the bottom half of your full swing. If your half-swing is good, it is much easier when you take a larger swing.

Start your full-swing practice with one of the shorter clubs in your bag (pitching wedge or 9 iron) and with some half-swings as well. Many golfers complain that they hit the ball OK on the range but then regress when they get to the golf course. A contributing factor in this unfortunate phenomenon is that they fail to make the driving range experience as much as possible like the golf course experience. Many ranges, especially the sophisticated new learning centers, feature target greens similar to what you will find on the golf course. They are greens, complete with flagsticks, framed by sand bunkers. Imagine you are playing a round of golf.

Alternate the clubs you hit. Rather than hitting 20 successive shots with the number 1 wood, which you would never do on the golf course, follow this method: First, select a target. Hit one drive. Select a target green and then choose an iron club. Align for the target green. Then choose a target for a pitch shot and adjourn to the practice putting green, hitting lag putts (long putts of 20 or more feet, trying to roll the ball close to the hole). Follow those with putts of 3 to 5 feet, preferably on a slope, so that you must play a break. Work on your distance control during this time.

Then return to the tee line and your mat and clubs and in your imagination play another hole, hitting in order, your 3 wood and 5 wood, followed by a full iron shot, a pitch shot, and then some putts.

Simply banging out all the balls in a bucket with one club, never aligning to a different target, is practice guaranteed not to follow you to the golf course. Using an alignment club during your practice may be very helpful in working on proper alignment on the golf course.

Another problem at the range, which you must learn to handle so it won't jeopardize your game, is unsolicited advice. Some driving range pros, trying to recruit pupils, will engage in a practice called in the trade dynamiting the tees. They'll saunter up and down the tee line, pausing momentarily at the station of a golfer who is obviously having problems. "Lemme give you a little tip," is a typical opening line. "OK," responds the struggling neophyte. What follows is often a barrage of advice, enough to inflict the dreaded paralysis by analysis. If the range teachers don't get into the act, some helpful amateur is sure to offer advice to the struggling ladies, particularly if they are young and attractive. As a new golfer you will be amazed at how much unsolicited advice you attract, most of it worth exactly what you paid for it. Because amateur advice can be hazardous to your golf swing I have included a detailed commentary on it. Try to ensure that your practice session has purpose. If your professional has given you specific practice drills, be sure to do them. The time you spend practicing will help supplement your lessons and thus will help your lesson time to be more productive.

End on a Good One!

Do not practice until you are so exhausted that your percentage of good shots plummets. Practice to a productive point, not to a point of exhaustion. And always end on a good shot. This will help you to remain positive. It is the good ones that keep you coming back.

Lesson 16
The Hazards of Amateur Advice—The Prince Charming Syndrome

One of the most difficult aspects of golf with which the beginning woman golfer must cope is well-meaning but unwanted advice from husbands and male friends who for some reason feel compelled to share with women of their acquaintance. Most teaching pros have had this experience.

I have spent many years studying the golf swing and how to teach it. Then, for example, I give a woman a lesson and she'll walk away and down to the end of the range, where her husband meets her and starts to work on her swing. I can tell by the positions he is putting her in that his advice is diametrically opposed to what I just told her. He is holding her head in a rigidly locked position. In our lesson I said nothing about "head down." I rarely do. That's because as your spine rotates in a counterclockwise direction on the follow-through, your head, being attached, naturally rotates or "comes up" along with it. And the more diligently a player tries to keep her head down, the more her head resists that effort by coming up. Yet "keep your head down!" is the most popular of all the advice amateurs pass along to hapless women. "Take a slow backswing!" is probably the next on the popularity list, right ahead of "Keep your left arm straight!"

We must be careful not to give advice that can easily be over-done. That is one of the greatest defects of amateur advice: It can easily be overdone. Slow backswings can turn into no backswings. Straight left arms can be hyperextended.

Probably the worst advice—and most peddled by the amateurs—is "keep your head down." Go to your local driving range and you'll see dozens of golfers fervently trying to keep their heads down, with the results that they're giving up their follow-through to do it. This is also a great way to injure your back.

You can gracefully handle this problem by telling the person who is trying to help you that you are working on what you learned in your last lesson and do not want to think about anything else at this point. This answer is truthful and to the point and will help to avoid confusion. You do want to limit the number of swing thoughts. A golf swing is over very quickly. You can probably only handle one or maybe two thoughts.

I've also witnessed the Prince Charming Syndrome on a first hand basis. My good friend and the PGA South Western Georgia Teacher of the Year, Terri Norris of Columbus, Georgia, was at a driving range in my hometown of Geneva, New York. Terri was fooling around hitting the golf ball, on purpose I might add, off the extreme heel of her club, so the ball would travel directly backward between her legs and pound against the wooden divider between the hitting stalls. It was all rather amusing! Then, saved by "Prince Charming," the guy in the next stall, who gave Terri a few tips, she started to hit the ball perfectly in the club face. Well, the advice was not good, but he felt as if he had saved the world, and we had a good time at his expense.

Accepting unsolicited advice is very dangerous. It will hinder your ability to improve because you are going to have to waste your time and effort undoing the damage. Cause and effect in the golf swing is a very complex subject. It takes a trained and educated eye. I have been teaching for 10 years. I see things now that I am sure I would not have recognized 5 years ago. I have had the opportunity to watch a lot of great teachers give lessons. I learn from them. I have learned an amazing amount working for Mike Adams the last three years. I learn every time I have the opportunity to watch another teacher teach. Todd Anderson, who is a PGA professional currently teaching at the Breakers in Palm Beach, is an excellent instructor, who has been nothing but cordial in allowing me to watch him teach. This is very common among PGA and LPGA teaching professionals. We learn from each other. But these are experienced instructors. Just because the person hitting next to you on the range is better than you does not mean that person will be able to help you.

Every club has their members who think they can teach. We had a member at Admirals Cove who constantly gave lessons to other members. This was great for our business. He would have them work on the same thing that he was working on. He did not and does not understand cause and effect. He would make the problem worse, so we would have to fix his damage.

A good teaching professional may spend up to 10 to 15 minutes with a student before attempting to implement corrections. How can Prince Charming in your Saturday foursome at Muni come up with a correction after watching only two swings? So save your golf game! Just tell these "Prince Charmings" that you like the pro you are working with and want to concentrate on the correction and fundamentals you are getting from him or her. My husband, Tim, is a PGA professional and a good teacher. He does help me from time to time, but only when I *ask* for help.

If your significant other feels compelled to help you, you

should schedule a lesson with your golf professional and have your would-be helper come along. That way he can know what to look for specifically in your swing so that he does not contradict what the professional and you are trying to do.

Significant others are not the only villains in this unwanted advice department. If you are paired with men at the golf course where you play, you'll get advice. I've been thinking of having a business-size card printed up that my students could give to their playing companions on the golf course. It would say:

> Thank you for resisting the urge to give swing advice to this woman. She is currently taking lessons from me. We'll appreciate your not adding to her confusion.
>
> KELLIE S. GARVIN
>
> *Class-A PGA Professional*
>
> *Class-A LPGA Professional*

Lesson 17
Playing a Round of Golf, Plus Etiquette

LESSON GLOSSARY

Ball mark: A small damaged area on the green caused by the ball, usually hit with an iron striking the green.

Executive course: A course shorter than regulation length to speed playing time.

Divot: A piece of turf dug up in hitting a ball, usually with an iron.

Fore: A word that is shouted to warn others that they need to cover their heads because they are in danger of being struck by an errant golf ball.

Greens fee: A fee paid for the use of the golf course.

Marshal: A person designated to keep players moving on the course and to make sure players adhere to required etiquette, particularly in regard to care of the course. Also known as a ranger.

Picking up: The discontinuation of play on a hole.

Starter: A person designated to start players playing in the order of their tee times.

Starting time: A time reserved for you and your group to start your round.

Playing a Round of Golf

Now you and your professional have declared your skills are adequate and your knowledge of rules and etiquette is sufficient that you may venture out for your first round of golf without your professional. Your pro recommends what is called an executive course. This will be shorter and therefore probably more manageable for your first experience.

Your first step is to obtain a starting time, or your tee-off time. The person answering the phone offers you a choice of, say, 10:20 or 12:45 and asks how many in your group. You choose 10:20, and you respond that there will be three of you playing. While you have a golf course employee on the line ask him about the dress code. He responds that you must wear Bermuda-length (longer) shorts and that men must wear collars on their shirts. No tank tops. No cutoffs. No short shorts. No jeans. You then go over to the checklist of things to bring that the pro gave you in your last group lesson.

Always check before you arrive at the first tee to be sure that you are prepared. Do not rely on others to be prepared for you. I always have my new students go into the golf shop every time before they tee off to prepare themselves with tees, ball markers, scorecard, and pencil.

My student Cheryl is so great at this. We have been working together for six years now. She is so prepared when she travels to the first tee that oftentimes she is ready before I am.

Things to Bring

•clubs

•balls (8 to 10 and previously owned are OK)

•sunscreen

•insect repellent

•Band-Aids

•safety pins

•golf towel

•sanitary products

•Kleenex

•ball markers

•lunch money

•aspirin

•antihistamine (for allergies and bugs)

This may all be combined in one small case, so that you can easily find what you need. You will be surprised at how often you or someone in your group tears out a hem and needs a safety pin or is rubbing a blister on her heel in her new golf shoes and needs a Band-Aid.

The necessary supplies.

Your greens fee, or fee for the use of the course, will be paid in the golf shop, where you also pick up a scorecard and a pencil. If you choose to ride in a cart, you will pay an extra fee.

It is a good idea to arrive early and hit a few balls to warm yourself up and to get a feel for the direction in which the ball is traveling that day. If you happen to be slicing it on the range that day, do not attempt to fix this on the golf course; simply aim left of center.

You will then make your way to the first tee, where there may or may not be a starter. The starter is a course employee whose job it is to get the golfers going on the first tee in sequence. The ranger or a marshal will keep you moving along on the golf course.

"On the tee, the 10:20 tee time," the starter will announce, and one of your group will volunteer to be the first to tee off. Nervous about her first golf adventure, she tees up with a 5 iron, because she has confidence in this club, and is surprised that the ball goes straight down the middle. If you swing and totally miss the ball, try to remain as calm as possible and simply try again. If you just dribble the ball off the tee, do not pick it up and retee, but rather move the ball up to where the others in your group are. If you retee, you slow down the pace of play for the entire group of people teeing off behind you.

Each member of your group, without dawdling, tees up and hits her tee shot and walks quickly off in the direction of the tee shots after all have hit. You will play in the order so that whoever is the farthest away from the hole is "away" and will be the next to hit. This process is continued throughout the hole until each of you has putted the ball into the hole. After each of the members of your group has holed out (putted the ball into the cup), you walk quickly over to the next tee, where you ask each what she shot. Then, sitting on the bench, you record the scores on the scorecard. Note that you always must be careful to walk off the previous green or even from a position behind the green before recording your scores, so as to not hold up the players behind you. This process will be continued on whatever number of holes you and your group choose to play.

The course marshal, seeing a group of women, inevitably tells them they must speed up to close the gap between them and the group ahead. It is your responsibility to keep up with the group just ahead of you. If there is an entire hole open in front of you and you are not able to catch up, simply pick up your balls and move up to just behind the preceding group's position. You should continue to do this as many times as necessary. Even in today's society, women are still always stereotyped as the slow players. Don't expect red carpets, and not expecting them, perhaps you will not be disappointed when you are not welcomed with one. Try also not to be startled when you learn that many men do not believe women should be on the golf course. Unfortunately, these men include some shop employees, as well as the greenkeeper, who appears convinced that the best day to aerate (put many little holes into the green to allow the grass roots to breathe) the greens is ladies' day.

To assist in the speed of play, attempt to play ready golf. However, do not risk life and limb to do this. Never walk in front of someone attempting to hit a golf ball. Ready golf really means that when it is your turn you are ready to hit. Women golfers appear obsessed with the necessity to play fast, their reputation as slow players haunting them. We have progressed from that point to a point where many of us rush excessively. So obsessive do these women club members become that they work themselves into a panic over the proximity of the foursome behind them. Stop looking behind you so often. Keep up with the group ahead of you and there's nowhere they can go.

I have to very often remind my students that if they are in position with the group ahead of them they do not need to turn around and check the group behind them every 30 seconds. Some of my students will even glance back after they have taken their setup to hit their shot just before they make their golf swing. This means that you are concentrating on the wrong thing. You need to be concentrating on the shot at hand and not the group behind you when it is your turn to hit. If you are distracted, start your routine again.

Women beginners who play slowly probably don't know how to play faster. There are techniques other than the obvious one of not hitting the ball so often. How do we accomplish this immediately? Just put the ball in your pocket after you have taken a previously determined number of swings on a hole. Ten is a fine round number; after you have taken 10 swings on a hole, pick the ball up and put it back into your pocket. This is called picking up, and unless you are playing in a major championship there is nothing cowardly or disgraceful about it.

Other time-savers are these:

•**Limit your practice swings to one.**

•**Be quick and decisive about what club you are going to**

hit on your next shot. This is a shot-making problem in which a yardage chart of the approximate distance you hit each club will be an aid.

•Be ready to hit when it is your turn. When the three other members of your foursome have hit their tee shots, you should be ready, glove on, tee club and ball in hand, to hit next.

•Limit the amount of time you search for golf balls. Does this mean if you lose a ball, as a beginner, you can't look for it? Not at all. If it is a new ball you lost, you sure do want to look for it. The first technique in looking for a lost ball is to mark it. That is, when you hit a ball that heads for the rough or the woods, note where it was last seen: third tree from the right on the fairway tree line; just past the 150-yard marker on the left of the fairway. Marking the balls of your playing partners so their lost balls may be located expediently also helps speed play. Otherwise, attempt to limit your search time to no more than one minute.

•Learn to walk quickly. If you want only a leisurely stroll, find the nearest public park and leash and walk your dog.

•Plan ahead. Leave your clubs or cart nearest to where you will be walking. This particularly applies around the greens. If the next hole you are playing is to your right, you will want to leave your clubs back right of the green, not front-left.

•Carry your ball washer with you. Rather than having to detour several yards to access a ball washer to remove the mud from your ball, keep a towel on your golf bag, one end wet, so as you are walking to the next hole you can be cleaning your golf ball.

Etiquette

The spectrum of golf etiquette may be very intimidating to women beginners, who may be so anxious to play ready golf they endanger their physical safety or trip over their own golf clubs to accomplish this goal. Ready golf means you agree to ignore the rules of golf, which in itself is against the rules, which dictate that the player farther from the hole shoots first. Ready? Shoot! Be sure before you hit that no one is ahead of you in a precarious position. The object of ready golf is to save time, but a spinning golf ball can be very dangerous. Golf etiquette can be categorized into two parts:

1. **Care of the course**

2. **Consideration of others**

1. Care of the Course

Care of the course etiquette advises that any damage you do to the golf course be repaired insofar as possible. Divots should be replaced, or if you are playing on a course where they provide you with sand and seed to be placed in the hole made by your iron swing, use the sand-seed mixture to start the growth of new turf in the divot hole. The divot hole is filled by the player with this mixture.

If your ball goes into a bunker, enter the bunker, with the rake in your hand, at the spot of shortest distance of sand to the ball, so you will have less area to rake, speeding up play. After you hit the shot, smooth all marks made during the shot. (Remember not to take a practice swing or set your club head against the ground in the bunkers!)

When an approach shot strikes a green, it usually leaves a ball mark, a small crater where the turf is destroyed, surrounded by a rim of grass, pushed up by the ball. If you do a good repair job on a ball mark, where the ball struck cannot be detected. Keep in mind that the ball mark will probably not be right next to your ball, but back where it initially landed on the green. Almost all beginners think that they never make a ball mark, but you do. One of my ladies hit a beautiful shot in one of her lessons. The 9 iron was a great shot. The ball traveled nice and high and landed on the green, producing a very large ball mark. I showed her the ball mark and told her that her golf ball had done this. It took me five minutes to convince her that she had made the mark. She felt that she was not good enough to make a ball mark, but in reality she certainly was. It is very important that you find the mark and fix it properly. Use either a tee or a ball mark repair tool; each is as good as the other. Insert the point just outside where the turf has been pushed up, and press the turf in toward the center of the mark. When the indentation made by the ball is covered, press the loose turf firmly down with the head of your putter or step on the damaged area. A putter does the job more effectively. You should, if the job has been done right, be unable to see the mark. An untended mark permits the grass to die eventually, and the mark will scar the green for a prolonged period. Moreover, ball marks without repair efforts are difficult to putt over.

Use a repair tool to repair all ball marks made on the putting green.

Tap down your repair job with your putter to smooth the surface.

2. Consideration of Others

Consideration of others includes an array of behaviors, as follows:

Be cautious you do not stand in another player's line of vision (including peripheral vision) while she is addressing the ball. Once you reach the putting green, make sure when you walk to your ball that you do not step in the line of any player's putt. This will hold true throughout the putting process.

Do not engage in conversation or make loud noises (such as dropping your bag of clubs) while someone else is hitting. You should not move, talk, or stand close when another player is making a stroke.

As I said before, the person who is the farthest from the hole is "away" and will be the first to putt. The player who is putting always has the option to putt out, as long as she keeps in mind not to step in the other player's line.

Offer to mark your ball if it is in the line of another player's putt. To mark a ball, place a very small coin, such as a dime, or a ball marker made for that purpose directly behind the ball, and then pick up the ball. To replace the ball, set it down slightly ahead of the marker and then pick up the marker and proceed to putt the ball.

A ball marker should be placed directly behind the ball, and then pick up the ball.

It is usually the obligation of the person whose ball is closest to the hole to attend the flagstick for the person who is putting if she requests it. ("Would you get the pin for me, please?") If there is a wind blowing, hold the flag against the stick, so it won't flap and distract the player. Hold the flagstick at arm's length, being careful your shadow does not fall across the cup and is on the same side of the cup as the shadow of the flagstick. Be cautious not to stand so close to the cup that you break down the edges of the cup. Keep the flagstick base loose in its place in the cup, as you will need to remove the flagstick as your playing companion's ball approaches it. There is a two-stroke penalty imposed should a ball strike the flagstick when it is in the cup if you are putting from on the green. The penalty is on the owner of the ball, not the person attending the flagstick.

Also, extend the same courtesy to others that you would want and remember that advice should only be given when asked for.

Golf Cart Consideration

When driving the golf cart be sure not to drive too close to the greens or the tee box. The cart should be no closer than 30 yards at any time. Often courses will have white lines or ropes to keep you from parking too close. If there is a cart path, try to use it as much as possible. When you approach the green to putt, park the cart toward the next tee and even with the green. Never park the cart back short of the green, because then you will have to walk back to get the cart and hold up the players behind you. Try to share the driving responsibilities, even if your bag is not on the driver's side. If your playing partner has a chip from in front of the green and your ball is already on the green, drop your partner off with her appropriate club to chip with and her putter and then pull the cart around. This will help keep play moving. Adhere to any cart rules determined by the conditions of the course. For example, if there has been a lot of rain, they may tell you, "Cart paths only." This means the cart is to remain on the path at all times. Take several clubs out to your ball with you, so you do not have to return to the cart to get another club. If the 90-degree rule is in effect, you will keep your cart on the path until you are even with your golf ball, then turn the cart 90 degrees to proceed straight to your ball. This will help minimize the amount of time the cart is on the grass. Park the cart to the right of a right-hand player, even with her golf ball. Do not pull the cart ahead of the ball. You should park between three to five yards to the right of her golf ball—close enough to make getting a club easy but not so close as to be in the way of the swing.

Driving the Golf Cart

If you can drive a car, you can drive a golf cart. It is actually very easy. First, insert the key and turn it to the on position. The cart will not move until you hit the gas, so do not be worried when you turn the key on. You can leave the key in the on position the entire time. It is not necessary to turn the key off when you stop the cart. The cart will not lose charge or gas unless the gas pedal is depressed. There will be a lever, normally located by the back of your legs, that puts the cart into gear, forward, neutral, or reverse. For the cart to travel forward, put the cart into forward gear by pushing the level to the forward direction. You will leave the lever in this position unless you want to travel backward. If you want to put the cart into reverse, simply move the lever to the reverse side. Most carts will make a beeping noise in reverse to let you know you are in reverse. To move the cart, simply depress the gas pedal. They normally do not start really fast, so do not be nervous. The cart will steer just like a car. You will find that the cart can turn in a relatively tight radius, so you can turn around easily in small areas. When you want to slow the cart, simply take your foot off the gas. When you want to stop the cart, take your foot off the gas and then slowly start to depress the brake. You will see a small parking brake in the corner of the brake pedal. When you park the cart, depress the parking brake so that it remains in its downward position, and this will hold the cart in its position on hills. When you go to restart the cart, you can simply press the gas pedal and the parking brake will automatically disengage.

This is a very quick description of how to drive a cart. It is not that difficult. You can ask your professional to show you how, and I am sure he or she will be happy to help.

For safety reasons, only attempt to drive the cart from the driver's side. Very recently a member of a local club attempted to drive the cart from the passenger side and caught her foot and ended up flipping the cart into a pond. She was very, very lucky not to hurt herself. Driving the cart is not difficult, but you do want to pay attention to what you are doing.

Keeping Score Can Be Fun

One suggestion on keeping score is just to make a mark for each good shot that you hit until such time as enough good shots are made to justify keeping the total score. Each time you go out to play, try to increase your total number of good shots. Nothing can spoil a pleasant day on the course so effectively as a scorecard and a pencil.

The rules of golf restrict players to a maximum of 14 clubs, usually enforced only in formal tournament play, but don't be surprised if some rules hawk on your ladies' day saunters over to your bag on the first tee to count your clubs. Usually in social rounds this restriction is overlooked, because the odds are overwhelming that you won't use all your clubs in one day's round and even if you did the advantage gained would be minuscule. Although different courses use different methods to display yardages and to indicate cup positions, there is some standardization. Some courses use yardage markers at the edge of the fairway, stakes on which may be marked distances to the green. Others use color coding—red stakes for 100 yards, white stakes for 150 yards, while blue stakes are used to tell you it is 200 yards to the green.

Sprinkler covers also may be used to show the exact yardage to the green—98 yards, 122 yards. These yardages are most often measured to the center of the green. So you will need to subtract yardage if the pin is in the front of the green and add yardage if the pin is located more toward the back. In addition, color differentiation—red, white, and blue—is used on flagsticks to show if the cup is cut near the front of the green, in the center, or in the back. Another method of showing cup position is large plastic whiffle balls placed on the flagstick. A ball placed on the lower third of the pin shows the cup position is in the front of the green, in the center of the flagstick shows center position, and in the upper third announces that the cup is in the back of the green.

Once you get your yardage and add or subtract yardage based upon the pin position in the green, it is also important to consider outside factors that will influence how far you do hit the ball as well as how far you need to hit the ball. The following are examples:

Downwind: The ball will travel farther; subtract distance from your calculated yardage.

Into the wind: The ball will travel a shorter distance; add to your calculated yardage.

Elevated green: You need to add distance to your calculated yardage.

Downhill to the green: You need to subtract distance from your calculated yardage.

Humidity: The ball will travel a shorter distance; add distance to your calculated yardage.

Over water: Add distance to your calculated yardage.

If most of your trouble is short of the green, add distance to your calculated yardage. Most amateurs tend to take too little club, expecting to hit the ball perfectly, and more times than not end up well short of their target. Once you reach a decision on the yardage that you want to hit the shot, consult your yardage chart and choose the appropriate club. Do not hesitate to take a little extra club, meaning a 5 iron rather than a 6 iron, for example. It is OK to miss the ball long of the green; there is usually less trouble over the green. This whole process should happen relatively quickly. Try to plan ahead as you are riding in the cart to your ball to save time when you get there.

One of my student's husbands tried to play so quickly she ended up with bruises on her legs from jumping from a moving cart. I think I would drive my own cart.

Nine Is Enough!

Do not feel that it is necessary to play 18 holes every time you go to play. I very often feel that nine holes are enough for me. It takes only two hours, which leaves me more time for the rest of my life. There are plenty of other golfers who will wish only to play nine with you as well.

Play a Scramble

A great format for beginners to play when they first travel to the golf course is the scramble. This is a team event in which the players in the group all tee off, the best shot of the group is chosen, and all players then hit from that chosen position. So if you hit a poor shot, you can pick the ball up and move it to the best ball. This process is continued, including putts, until the ball is holed. This is really a fun way to play, and it allows you to keep your pace of play moving.

On Course Strategy

You do not always need to tee off with your driver. When you hit your first shot on any hole, you should be hitting a club with which you are comfortable. Let's assume you are playing a 340–yard par four. You would hit the physically longest club you are comfortable with from the golf tee. It may be your 7 wood or even your 5 iron. So you tee off with your 7 wood and you hit the golf ball 120 yards. You then have 220 yards remaining. Normally you will be more comfortable hitting a longer club from the tee than from the ground. For example, I might be comfortable hitting my 5 wood from the tee, but the longest club I might hit from off the ground is a 5 iron or 7 wood. You will then hit the physically longest club that you are comfortable hitting from the ground without the golf tee. In many cases for beginners the 5 iron is a great choice here. The 5 iron is a good balance between a club that is short enough that it feels manageable, yet long enough that you would be able to hit the ball a respectable distance. You will continue with the 5 iron until the distance you have left to the hole is less than you can hit the 5 iron in a full swing. I then hit two 5 irons that each traveled 80 yards. I have hit the ball 280 yards to this point and I have 60 yards remaining. I would then refer to my yardage chart and see that my 8 iron travels 60 yards so that would be my club of choice. I hit my 8 iron well, but it ends up just left of the green. I will then decide whether to chip or pitch the ball, based upon whether I need more time in the air (pitch), or is it OK to roll the ball the majority of the way to the cup (chip). Once on the green I will then putt until the ball is holed. This is a good example of how to manage the golf course. If my tee shots with my wood are going very well, I may then choose to graduate myself to a longer club on the next tee shot, a 3 wood rather than a 5 wood. If I were having trouble with my 5 iron on the fairway, I would choose a physically shorter club like a 6 or 7 iron just to receive some positive feedback of some solid contact. Airborne and forward 70 yards is much better than dead sideways 90 yards.

Tee up on the side of the trouble. If there is water on the right side of the hole, tee your ball up on the right side of the tee. It is easier to aim away from the trouble and will open the left side of the hole up to you visually.

Tee up on the side of the trouble, so you can aim away.

If your ball is off the putting surface, but the grass is short and consistent, do not hesitate to putt. You do not have to be on the green to putt. Putting is forgiving and will help keep the potential embarrassment factor low.

In a situation on the golf course that you are totally clueless as to how to handle, after a couple failed attempts do not hesitate to pick your golf ball up and put it back onto the fairway, provided that you are not playing in a tournament. This will help you keep up the pace of play, as well as maintain your sanity and your enjoyment. The goal is to have a good time, is it not?

Play the percentages. If a flagstick is tucked behind a bunker, aim for the center of the green. Do not expect a perfect shot. Play for the path of least resistance.

Do not attempt to change your swing on the golf course. Play for the shot pattern that you are hitting that day. For example, if you are slicing the ball, aim more to the left. Save the corrections for the range with your professional.

Try to have a good time at all costs. This is the purpose of your being on the course!

Teeing the Ball

How To

As a beginner you will spend a lot of your practice time teeing the golf ball up. You will waste a lot of time and look like a beginner if you do not place the ball on the tee properly. If the tee is crooked, the ball will continually fall off the tee onto the ground

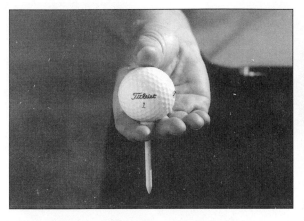

Above: Cradle the ball in your palm with the tee between your index and middle fingers.

Right: Bend forward, and place the tee into the ground with the ball already on the tee.

and drive you crazy. Place the tee in between your index and middle fingers with the point facing out and the cup for the ball facing in toward your palm. Cradle the ball in the palm, so that the ball rests in the cup of the tee. Bend forward and put the tee straight into the ground with the ball already on the tee.

How High

On the golf course we want to tee the ball at different heights based upon the club we are using. For an iron shot on a par 3, for example, you should tee the ball relatively low. For a fairway wood being hit off a tee, a 5 wood for example, you will want to tee the ball slightly higher. For a driver (1 wood) you will want to tee the ball even higher. Everyone uses a slightly different height to tee the ball. With the woods, the larger the club head, the higher you will want to tee the ball. Approximately one-half to three quarters of the ball should be over the top of the club head. When you are playing a round of golf you are permitted by the rules only to place the ball on a tee for the first shot on each hole.

Tee the ball low for irons.

Tee the ball medium for fairway woods.

Tee the ball high for the driver, so about half the ball is over the top of the club head.

Technically you are not allowed to tee the ball up in the fairway. Although I would say to you if you are having a day from hell and nothing is working and you have to place the ball on a tee in the fairway, go ahead and do so, provided that you are not playing in a tournament, as that would not be legal. If it takes this adjustment to have a good time, make it.

One of my favorite students, Cheryl, was a perfect example of when and how to tee the ball. The first year we worked together, she would only hit irons on the golf course and would tee up almost every full shot. The second year, she would hit her irons from off the ground and would hit her tee shot only with her 7 wood. When she had trouble with her 7 wood on her tee shots, she would return to her 5 iron off the tee. The third year she, would hit her irons and her 7 wood from off the ground and would tee off with either her 7 wood or her 5 wood. The fourth year, she was able to hit all of her fairway woods from off the ground and teed up with her 3 wood. This order of progression was great. She can now hit the ball farther than a lot of the ladies she hoped to be able to comfortably play with are able to hit it. Now we have to work on her short game! I am very proud of her.

For Practice
Should you tee the ball up when you practice? Start your practice on a tee. As you hit shots that progress into the air, start to tee the

ball lower. If the ball is teed very low and is going into the air and you are knocking the tee out of the ground, go ahead and hit shots off the grass. Try to ensure that you have a good lie, meaning that the ball is not sitting in a hole, when you place it onto the ground. Practice off the ground until you run into trouble, with several misses in a row, and then move back to the tee. Once the tee starts coming out of the ground again, return to hitting balls from the grass only. This practice order will challenge you yet allow you to remain positive during your practice time.

Oftentimes many of my beginners feel they are "cheating" if they are practicing from off a tee. This is not the case. While you are learning, it is much more important that you work on the correct fundamentals, rather than having to worry about how the ball is sitting. Mike Adams often points out to his students that even professional golfers practice from a tee, as well as professional baseball players practicing their hitting fundamentals from a tee.

Lesson 18
Bunkers: Green Side, Fairway, and Buried Lies

LESSON GLOSSARY

Bunker: A depression in the golf course, often filled with sand.

Explosion: A shot hit out of sand in which the club strikes only the sand, and usually much sand. The sand moves the ball from the bunker.

Fairway bunker: A bunker located near a fairway that is farther away from the target than you can hit the ball splashing sand.

Green side bunker: A bunker located beside a green.

Pot bunker: A small, symmetrical round bunker, on either a fairway or a green side.

Trap: Another name for a bunker.

Green Side

For some reason, many women seem to fear the bunker. You can be a successful bunker player if you simply follow a few correct fundamentals and learn to splash the sand.

The invention of the sand wedge is thought to be to golf what the invention of the airplane was to modern transportation. For centuries, golfers had been trying to extricate their golf balls from sand bunkers with inadequate weapons, such as the pitching wedge and the 9 iron. Both clubs dug into the sand. Sand shots terrorized golfers, and particularly women golfers, who lacked the strength to move large amounts of sand *and* the ball. Then the sand wedge appeared on golf shop shelves. Its innovative design can best be viewed in profile. Note that the leading edge of the sand wedge is lower than the center of the sole. This design assures that the rounded sole will skip across the sand, rather than digging in. This is called bounce. From a green side bunker you will probably have no more than 30 yards to go, and yet you will be taking a full swing, because the swing will be taking sand with the ball. I realize that it may be difficult to convince yourself to take such a full swing when the target is so close, but you must. It is the force of the sand against the ball that moves it. The objective is to reach the bottom of your swing arc before reaching the ball. Therefore, you will position yourself so the ball is opposite the instep of your left heel, as for a teed wood shot. This ball position allows you to contact the sand first, and the splashing of the sand moves the ball out of the bunker. If you contact the ball first, the result will be a skulled shot, in which the ball is partially topped. A skulled shot will go far past the flagstick, perhaps over the green, or will hit the lip of the bunker and stay in the sand. You should also wiggle your feet down into the sand to help you hit the sand and not the ball. Practice splashing only the sand

Take a full backswing for green side bunkers.   Take a full forward swing for green side bunkers.

without golf balls to start. If you are unable to splash the sand, wiggle your feet down lower into the sand. This will help you work on the motion, rather than worrying about the ball. It is a full swing back and through, so you should be splashing a lot of sand out of the bunker and onto the green. After you successfully practice splashing the sand, add a small rock or a golf tee. Place either on the top of the sand and practice splashing the sand out from around the tee or small rock. You should notice that the momentum of the sand will also carry the rock or tee out of the bunker and onto the putting surface. When you are in the bunker, you are not allowed to ground your club. In other words you are not allowed to set the sole of the club down into the sand

Above: Position the ball more forward in your stance for your bunker shots so you will be able to connect with the sand before the ball.

Right: Splash the sand. The club head should never contact the ball, only the sand.

behind the golf ball. I would like you to consider, however, actually taking a practice swing before hitting your sand shot and practicing splashing the sand out of the bunker and onto the green. This would be against the rules of golf, but it would teach you to be a better bunker player quicker.

To vary the length of the shot, always taking a full swing, you will vary the amount that you open the club face. As you open the club face more, adding more loft to the club, this will result in a higher shot, landing more softly on the green. To open the club face, rotate the shaft and the grip of your club clockwise. Then replace your hands on the grip. Rotating the grip while keeping your hands in place avails you nothing. The shorter the shot, the more you will open the face. There is some stance compensation necessary, because when you open the club face it also aims more to the right. The more you open the club for shorter shots, the more the club face aims to the right. To offset this you will want to align your body more to the left and thus realign the club face to the target.

Many women discover that they do not need to open the club face excessively, and some not at all. If you open the face too much, the ball will travel too short of a distance and will not travel outside the bunker. I would recommend that you start with your first bunker shots with everything square to the target, including the club face and your body lines parallel to the target line. Our first goal is just for you to be able to get the ball out of the bunker. We can work on distance control as you go.

Now find a practice bunker, and many of the upscale practice centers do have them. Focus on practice swings that splash

The openness of the club face will control the distance, slightly open to normal for longer shots.

More open for medium length shots.

Very open for short shots.

sand. Then progress to splashing sand to move golf balls. Once you are successful in getting the golf balls out, add a target and work on your distance control by varying the amount you open your club face.

Summary

1. Take a full swing.

2. Place the golf ball forward in your stance or more toward your left foot.

3. Wiggle your feet down into the sand.

4. Splash the sand.

5. Vary the amount you open the club face to control your distance. Short shot: Club face very open. Medium shot: Club face open. Long shot: Club face only slightly open.

Fairway

Most fairway bunker shots must be hit very differently from green side bunker shots. The lip or the face of the bunker must be given serious consideration, because you may not be hitting this shot with a sand wedge and not with an open face. You must use enough loft to hit the ball over the face of the bunker, based upon your club selection. If you have become quite skilled with your irons, a 7 or 8 iron might be a feasible club. Above all, your goal should be to emerge from the bunker and advance the ball as far toward the green as possible, with minimal risk. A fairway bunker is a pick clean shot. This means little or no sand. You will be taking your normal full swing. The keys to a fairway bunker are (1) narrowing your stance and (2) gripping down on the club. Wiggle your feet only slightly

For fairway bunker shots, narrow your stance and lower your hands on the grip of the club.

into the sand for stability of the stance. The results of these modifications are your becoming taller, your club becoming shorter, and the elimination of some lower body motion. Ball position is based upon the club you are hitting, similar as it would be off grass. You may wish to move the ball position more to the right in your stance. This will help you to contact the ball before the sand. You do, however, want to try to avoid moving the ball position too far left in your stance, which may cause you to hit the sand first, which is not preferable. If a narrowed stance and a grip down on the club do not result in a cleanly hit (no sand taken) shot, try a stance that is even more narrow and grip down farther on the club. If you still continue to take too much sand, try looking at the top half of the ball. If the lip of the bunker is very shallow, you might successfully try a 6 iron from the bunker. Beginners are ill advised to use a wood from a fairway bunker; this is a very advanced shot.

Summary

1. **Choose an iron with enough loft to easily clear the lip of the bunker.**

2. **Narrow your stance.**

3. **Grip down on the club.**

4. **Move ball position slightly to the right in your stance.**

5. **Take a normal golf swing.**

Buried Lies

Occasionally a shot coming out of the air and landing in a bunker will bury its own pitch mark. This can also be called a fried egg. It looks much more intimidating than it is in reality. With a couple of setup changes you can extricate the ball from the bunker, hopefully somewhere on the putting surface.

Play the ball slightly back in your stance. This will cause the club face to de-loft and will turn your sand wedge into more of a digger, which will help you dig the ball out of the bad lie. This will promote hitting the shot on the downswing. Your weight should favor the left foot and stay on your left side throughout the full swing. Take a full backswing and hit very aggressively down. The club will be very steep in its angle of attack into the sand, so expect your follow-through to be minimal, if any, as the sand will stop the momentum. The swing should feel steep up and down. The angle the club takes into the sand is the angle at which the ball will come out of the sand. The motion may feel like that of a chop because it is so steep.

Summary

1. Play the ball position back in your stance.

2. Leave your weight on your left foot.

3. Take a full backswing, and swing steeply down into the sand.

My students are often amazed at how simple this shot is with the correct setup and the steep angle of attack. The expression on a student's face when the ball pops right out of the buried lie looks like she just saw a magic trick. Keep in mind here that with the buried lie your goal is just to recover and to get the ball out of its precarious position. It is more difficult to control distance.

Lesson 19
Irregular Lies

You won't play golf very long before you discover the game is not played on the level! Even in Florida there is mounding beside those flat fairways and you'll be playing on uphills, downhills, and sidehills with your feet above the ball and sidehills with your feet below the ball.

General Compensations and Questions for Sidehill Lies

A sidehill lie is a lie when the ball is not on the same level as your feet. There are two questions that you should ask yourself when making your adjustments in your setup. The purpose of questions is to help you to remember the necessary adjustments. It is easier to remember when you understand what you are trying to accomplish, rather than trying to just memorize.

Question #1: If I were to pour a bucket of water on the ball, which way would it flow? The direction the water would flow in relationship to your target is the direction in which the ball will tend to fly. Whatever the hill does, the ball will tend to do.

Question #2: Is the golf ball closer or farther away from me than it would be if it were in a flat lie?

Sidehill Lie with the Ball Above Your Feet

Answer #1: The water would flow to the left, in relationship to the target, so it will be necessary for you to aim more to the right, because the ball will tend to fly to the left from this lie. How much to align right depends upon the severity of the slope, and only experience can teach you how much sidehill produces how much pull.

Answer #2: The ball is closer to you than in a flat lie; you must therefore grip down on the club, or you will hit the ground before the ball. Take a practice swing. (One should be enough!) If you hit the ground excessively on your practice swing, grip even lower on the club.

For a side hill lie with the ball above your feet, place your hands lower on the grips and aim more to the right of your target.

For a side hill lie with the ball below your feet, step closer to the ball and aim left.

Sidehill Lie with the Ball Below Your Feet

Answer #1: The water would flow to the right, in relationship to the target, so it will be necessary for you to aim more to the left to allow for a push.

Answer #2: The ball is farther away from you. Step in closer to the ball. Be sure to maintain your knee flex throughout the swing.

Two general precautions on sidehill lies: Swing within yourself. That is, never try to hit the ball harder than you would from a level lie. Also, as the lie is more severe, hit a physically shorter club, 7 iron for example, to help you maintain your balance.

General Compensations for Uphill and Downhill Lies

Uphill Lies

An uphill lie is one in which your left foot is higher than your right. Always match your shoulders to the slope on a uphill lie. Your left shoulder will be higher than your right. When you tilt your body to match the slope, this will increase the loft in the club face, causing the ball to go higher and travel less distance. The ball does what the hill does. The hill slopes up like a ramp, producing a higher ball flight. You may want to take a less-lofted club to offset this, a 5 iron rather than a 7 iron, for example. You will be swinging against gravity, due to the uphill, so you may want to move the ball slightly back in your stance to help you get through the shot. You should finish with your weight on your left foot as you would in a normal golf swing, even though you are fighting against the gravity of the hill.

My students seem to find it helpful to imagine the uphill lie as a ramp. The ball will go higher because of the slope of the hill.

On an uphill lie your shoulders should match the slope of the hill, expecting a higher than normal ball flight.

On an uphill lie, your weight should still finish on your left side as it would in a normal full swing.

Downhill Lies

A downhill lie is one where your left foot is lower than your right. Always match your shoulders to the slope on a downhill lie. Your left shoulder will be lower than your right and should maintain this position throughout the swing. When I tilt my body to match the slope, this will decrease the loft in the club face, causing the ball to be lower and roll more when it lands. You may

want to take a more lofted club to offset this, a 7 iron rather than a 5 iron for example.

I have found that beginners have difficulty remembering what the adjustments are for irregular lies, so I suggest you clip out "Summary of Uneven Lies," take it to a copy center, and have it laminated. Then punch a hole in the corner so you can tie it on your golf bag along with your yardage chart. Refer to it on irregular lies.

Practice uneven lies also on very short shots. On uphill and downhill your club should follow the contour of the slope as you swing. Practicing this is easier with a short iron, such as a 9 iron, on quarter-shots.

In my experiences I have found that each student will find one or two of the lies that she prefers and one or two with which she just is not comfortable. I try to schedule at least one or two clinics per year to work on uneven lies so that my students can review the necessary setup changes every so often. Be sure to practice the lies that you are not comfortable with so that you will feel more at ease on the golf course.

On a downhill lie, your shoulders should match the slope throughout the entire stroke, expecting a lower than normal ball flight.

Summary of Uneven Lies

LIE	STANCE ADJUSTMENT	ALLOW FOR	TAKE MORE/LESS LOFT
Sidehill, ball; above feet	Ball closer to you; grip down on club	A pull; align right	Same loft as flat lie
Sidehill, ball; below feet	Ball farther from you; step closer	A push; align left	Same loft as flat lie
Downhill	Weight on left side; shoulders match hill	lower ball, flight	A more-lofted club
Uphill	Shoulders match hill; if severe, move ball right in stance	higher ball, flight	A less-lofted club

Lesson 20
Bad Lies

What do I do differently if my ball is in a bad lie? First, let's define what is considered to be a bad lie. A bad lie is when the ball sits down deep, so that it is difficult to get the club down to the ball, or any other situation in which you think you will have a hard time getting the club head down to the ground. It is necessary to get the club down to the bottom of the ball in order to get the ball into the air. Several examples of bad lies are a ball in deep rough, a ball in deep rough around the edges of the green, a ball in a divot, a ball buried in the bunker, and a ball on hard pan. Although these situations are different, the adjustments you make are the same. This adjustment that you make may be specific more to women than to men, due to the fact that, unfortunately, most of us are not as strong as the men, so that it is harder to force the ball out of the bad lie. Make the following adjustments and you will be successful.

Do not assume that because a ball is in the rough it is in a bad lie. If the ball sits on top of the grass, this is very often a good lie even though the ball is in the rough. My student Judy seemed to not understand this. She always wanted to hit her 9 iron when she was in the rough. She was costing herself strokes because of the sacrifice of distance in hitting the 9 iron, rather than the 7 wood, which would have been fine out of good lies in the rough. Learn from Judy and evaluate the situation before assuming that you need to try to play so conservatively.

Your club selection should be a more lofted iron. The increased loft will help to extract the ball up and out of the bad lie.

The key to getting the ball out of a bad lie is positioning the ball more back in your stance—in other words, closer to being in line with your right foot. This will put your ball in a position where the golf club is still on the downward path of the circle. This descending motion will allow you to hit the ball first, rather than allowing any of the thick grass to slow the club head down. Any time you play the ball back in your stance, you will want to put your hands slightly lower on the grip of the club. Since the ball is back in your stance and you always want to let your arms hang naturally, the shaft of the club will be slightly angled to the left. Although the club head is in line with your right foot, the end of the grip of the club will

A golf ball is considered to have a bad lie when it sits down deep into the grass, where it is difficult to get the bottom of the club down to the bottom of the ball.

Position the ball back in your stance, more in-line with your right foot.

Hit straight down with momentum into the ground to extract the ball.

be in line with your left pocket on your pants. Your intention should always be to hit down and through the shot. In a chipping situation where you apply this, the ground may stop the forward momentum of your club, inhibiting your follow-through. Do not anticipate this, but rather if it happens let it, so that you do not intentionally slow down at impact. When you play the ball back in your stance the club face will be de-lofted, causing the ball to come out lower and roll more.

If you are still having trouble with tough lies, you may also try putting more weight onto your left foot and leaving it there. This will tilt your shoulders so that your left shoulder is lower, giving you a steeper angle of the club into the ball, pinching the ball out of the bad lie. This change in setup will allow you to hit the ball first and then the ground. You will avoid the thick grass or the problem by hitting in more of a descent on the ball rather than a circular sweeping motion.

Start with the smaller motion of a chip and work your way up to a full swing with this. You will have to hit the ground in order to be successful with this shot. Do not be afraid to make the mess when you hit the ground and kick up some grass and dirt.

The third hole at Atlantic is a par 4 with a necessary carry over long-fescue rough of approximately 120 yards to the fairway. This hole reeks havoc. By teaching the ladies to take a more lofted club and make the necessary setup adjustments I have made this hole no longer so intimidating to a lot of them.

Lesson 21
How to Choose an Instructor

When choosing an instructor there are several factors to consider, especially for women. A couple I teach, whom I'll call Tony and Patsy, had given up the game, but, and fortunately, decided to give it another try. With a little bit of extra time and effort to make them comfortable in their learning atmosphere I have helped make them the biggest fans of the game. They have bought their own golf cart, are always trying new golf clubs, and even decorated one of their bathrooms in their house with golf as the theme. Now, the game hadn't changed, but their comfort level had. Your instructor is very important in helping you feel comfortable. If you are not comfortable with your instructor, try another.

I believe personality to be one of the most important factors in helping you to choose an instructor or instructional program. You must trust that your instructor has your best interests at heart and choose a person whom you feel comfortable with. Word of mouth is often one of the best methods for choosing an instructor. If a friend with a similar disposition and personality loves his or her instructor, I would say that he or she would definitely be worth a try. Two characteristics of a teacher that I feel are very important for you to know are whether the instructor is a PGA or LPGA member and whether he or she is a good communicator. It is very important that your instructor has both training and the ability to apply this training.

You do not have to be a member of a golf club to receive high-quality instruction. Almost all private clubs allow their instructors to give lessons to nonmembers. Call the golf club to find out their policy. You can hit range balls. Often the quality of the practice facility will be higher than that of a driving range. Keep in mind that you will probably not have to pay for the practice balls as you would at a driving range. I am *not* trying to steer you away from driving ranges, because the quality of many ranges today is amazing. This is one area in the golf business that has changed drastically for the better. Just please check the credentials and experience of the teachers.

Money is also an important consideration. If you have unlimited funds, take as much instruction as you feel necessary, trying to always practice in between lessons, as long as your instructor recommends practicing. You can save money by taking clinics as well as group lessons. This will be less expensive, but remember you will be receiving less one-on-one instruction and not receiving the constant feedback you would receive in a private lesson. Another way to save money would be working with the assistants, rather than the head professional or lead instructor. Often the assistants' rates will be less expensive. If you are trying to conserve money, a good schedule is as follows: Take a half-hour lesson ($25–$60) every week, asking your instructor to set a practice schedule for you as well as very specific goals you must achieve before your next lesson.

Do not be late for your lesson. If you are comfortable hitting balls on your own, arrive 10 to 15 minutes early and warm up in the order discussed earlier. If you are so new that you are not comfortable hitting by yourself, just wait quietly somewhere within the sight of the instructor, but not too close. If the instructor is giving a lesson do not interrupt. When the lesson is complete he or she will be looking for you and appreciate your promptness and courtesy. The more you put into your golf, the more you will get out of your golf.

Lesson 22
Taking Lessons—How to Get the Most for Your Time and Effort

The time you spend with your professional is very important. In order to learn and improve, here are several suggestions to get the most out of your lessons.

Do not be afraid to ask questions. The only stupid question is the unasked, therefore unanswered, question. You may also want to express any difficulties that you have been having in your practice sessions at the beginning of the lesson. Your feedback really helps the instructor to assist you. This can also influence the structure of the lesson.

The number-one factor in getting the most from your lesson is *listening* and paying attention. It is not necessary to hit golf balls the entire time. It is more important to stop, listen, and learn. "What your mind conceives your body can achieve." You must understand what you are trying to make better and why. This is the first step you must take before you will improve.

The next most important factor to maximize improvement is patience. For some this is more difficult than others. Even if the changes you are making do not work immediately, *stick with them!* Do not jump ship in the middle of the ocean. Keep trying, and you will accomplish your goals.

A perfect example of sticking with it is a woman named Annette whom I used to teach at Admirals Cove and just recently returned to me for lessons because she was not improving anymore. We had a half-hour lesson that consisted of my trying to convince her of the necessary changes and her telling me how strange everything I suggested felt.

She called me three days later to tell me that she had gone out to play the next day and tried to do what I had suggested for four holes and it did not work, so she went back to her old way. My heart was broken.

She then returned one and one-half weeks later for another lesson. She started by making these perfect swings doing exactly everything I had suggested she do. I was so shocked I could barely speak. I then asked her what had happened. She said she *finally* realized that her way did not work and decided to stick with the changes. She was thrilled. I was thrilled. Her playing partners and her friends were amazed. She lowered her scores by over 15 strokes. She had improved because her attitude improved. Her decision to stick with the changes, even though they felt uncomfortable, allowed her to achieve this success. I am very proud of her.

Keep in mind that if it does not feel different, you have not changed anything; therefore, you should not expect to improve.

If any practice drills are given to you, do them. This will help your new ideas turn to habits quicker.

Always write down what you learned at the end of each lesson. This way you can always look back into your notes if you cannot remember everything or also if you run into the same problem at a later date.

As a golf professional, I want you to do *great!* Nobody is great all the time. It is more important to me that you are learning, rather than worrying about every shot. Do not worry if you totally miss the ball during your lesson. I believe it takes letting go of control in order to get better. Once again, do not be afraid to totally miss the ball. Do your best to do what is asked of you. Stick with it, and you will improve.

I take tennis lessons. As I love tennis, I thoroughly enjoy my lessons. I believe that taking these lessons helps me in my teaching golf. First of all, in tennis I cannot improve unless I understand what I am doing incorrectly and what I must do differently to make the changes. I ask a lot of questions. My instructor, Brenda, is a great instructor because she is a good communicator. She also realizes that in order for a student to improve she must focus on one problem, rather than skipping all over the place.

I also realize, because I teach golf and was also a beginner golfer at one point in my life, that just because I understand the necessary change does not mean that I can execute that change on a regular basis without repetition and feedback. This provides me with endless patience with my tennis as well as with my golf teaching. It takes time and perseverance to make a change. It sure is fun when the improvement starts to show. My forehand is so much better now!

Repetition

The sports psychologist Rick Jensen, who works with the golf school at PGA National, tells a story to the students of Nick Price wearing out the faces of three 9 irons in one season trying to make one small change in his swing. This is the epitome of repetition, which is necessary for change.

Lesson 23
The Rules You Need to Know

The rules are very numerous. Included here are the basic rules you need to know to get started. The rules are much more formal than the way I have explained them here, and in many cases there are more options than the one I have listed in each case. As you progress to an advanced stage, in which you play in tournaments, take the time to gain a solid working knowledge of the rules. There are many more rules than the ones listed, but these are the most commonly used.

Watch out for the rules hawks at your club. Some of them do know the rules, but many of them think they know the rules and do not. You will want to learn the rules out of respect for golf history. Remember to be kind to those who do not know. We were all beginners at one point.

I remember when I was a junior golfer at Seneca Lake Country Club the golf professional, Phil Louvier, made sure that each of us knew the rules.

The Teeing Ground

The teeing ground consists of the line between the two tee markers, extending back two club lengths. So it will normally form a rectangle. Do not tee off in front of the markers. That will give you away as a novice golfer.

The tee ground consists of the line between the tee markers, extending back two club lengths.

A ball accidentally knocked off the tee at its address should be replaced with no penalty.

Ball Knocked off the Tee at Address

When a ball is inadvertently knocked off of the tee at the address, replace the ball with no penalty. Beginners think that knocking the ball off the tee is a beginner thing to do and often become embarrassed when this happens. Even golf professionals knock the ball off the tee inadvertently, so don't worry when you do.

Sprinkler Heads

When your ball comes to rest on a sprinkler head or the sprinkler head interferes with your stance or your swing, you may take a free drop off the sprinkler head, no closer to the hole.

Above: You receive a free drop if a sprinkler head interferes with your stance and swing.

Right: Extend your arm out to shoulder height and drop the ball from your hand.

Bunkers

You are not permitted to ground your club in the bunker. In other words, you may not set your club down so that it touches the sand behind the ball. You must elevate the club over the sand until you make the swing, and then it is OK to touch the sand.

When my beginners are first learning to come out of the sane I do not want them to

Do not ground your club in the bunkers or the hazards.

worry about this. First work on the motion of splashing the sand, and you can worry about not grounding your club later.

Water Hazards

Yellow Stakes

When you hit your golf ball into a hazard marked with yellow stakes and you choose not to attempt to hit the ball, or cannot hit the ball, under penalty of one stroke, you drop the ball behind the hazard, keeping the point where the ball last crossed the line of the

When you hit your ball into a yellow-staked hazard, under penalty of one stroke you drop the ball behind the hazard, keeping the point where the ball last crossed the hazard between you and the hole.

When you hit your ball into a red-staked lateral hazard, under penalty of one stroke, you drop the ball within two club lengths of the point the ball last crossed the line between the hazard stakes.

hazard between you and the hole. So if I hit a ball and it lands across a yellow hazard, then bounces and comes back toward me into the hazard, I must still hit from the longer side of the hazard, because I must keep that point between the hole and myself. I can never drop the ball closer to the hole than where it ended up.

Red Stakes

Red stakes denote a lateral hazard. The easiest way to remember this is that the word *lateral* has the letter *r* in it for "red." A lateral hazard will normally run along the side of the hole. When you hit your ball into a lateral hazard and you cannot or choose not to try to play the ball from within the hazard, under penalty of one stroke, you drop your ball within two clubs lengths of the point where the ball last crossed the line of the hazard. If you choose to try to play the ball from within the hazard, you are not allowed to ground your club. In other words, you are not allowed to set the club on the ground. You must elevate the club off the ground until you make the swing, as in sand bunkers.

Out-of-Bounds

Out-of-bounds is labeled with white stakes. Your ball is out-of-bounds when all of it is outside the line between the stakes. The penalty for out-of-bounds is stroke and distance. To remember this, *out-of-bounds* consists of three words and *stroke and distance* is three words. So if I tee off and hit my ball out-of-bounds, I must retee the ball from my original position and add a stroke. So my score would be one

A ball is out of bounds when all of it lies outside the line between the stakes. The penalty is stroke and distance.

for the original ball, one penalty stroke, and my retee would be my third shot. So I would have three strokes to that point. Do not go up to the point where your ball went out-of-bounds and drop a ball there. You will look like a beginner if you do so. Out-of-bounds is a very expensive penalty, so try to avoid those little white stakes.

Lost Ball

I permit myself to search for a lost ball for up to five minutes, but I highly recommend against searching for this long. Take a quick look and if you do not find the ball move on. The penalty for a lost ball is the same as for out-of-bounds, stroke and distance, so if I lose my ball I must return to the position from which I hit it to its lost status and add a penalty stroke.

It is amazing to me the lengths to which people will go to recover a lost ball. I have seen 70-year-old ladies climb on their hands and knees on unstable rocks to grab that little golf ball wedged down by the water. Take my word for it—recovering a lost ball is not worth the risk of hurting yourself.

Provisional Ball

In an effort to speed up play, if I believe my ball to be out-of-bounds or lost I can hit a provisional ball from my original position to save me the time of having to walk back if my ball does turn out to be unplayable. I must declare my intentions before I do so. For example: "I believe my ball is out-of-bounds; I am going to hit a provisional ball." Your provisional ball should be a different-numbered ball or otherwise marked differently so you can identify the balls individually.

Unplayable Lie

If I hit my ball into a position where I believe I cannot hit or advance the ball, I have the option under one penalty stroke to take a relief two club lengths from the position of the ball. I can drop two club lengths to the side, either way, or two club lengths back. To drop the ball properly, I extend my arm at shoulder level, holding the ball in my fingers, and release it from my hand. You must never drop closer to the hole in any of these situations. If the ball bounces closer to the hole, redrop.

If you decide your ball is unplayable, under penalty of one stroke, you may drop the ball within two club lengths, no closer to the hole.

Lesson 24
Club Fitting—How Do You Know What Club's Right for You?

Club fitting has become such an exact science lately. Almost all of the larger club manufacturers are coming out with extensive fitting systems, and many businesses are opening around the country that will retool your clubs to make them fit you properly.

I still subscribe to a certain extent to the old "if you hit it well, buy it" theory. Here I will, however, attempt to give you a more scientific answer.

Women over the years have been forced to play with men's clubs, often too heavy and too long. The proper fit of equipment can be a big help. Women obviously come in different shapes and sizes. So should their equipment.

First, we must determine the appropriate length of the clubs. This will be based upon the length of the player's arms. You will want to hit the longest clubs with which you are still able to make relatively consistent contact with the center of the club face. If a club is too long, it will be very difficult to hit the ball with any consistency.

The proper lie angle of the club for you will also need to be determined. This is the angle at which the shaft of the club comes out of the club head. You can determine this by hitting balls off a board with tape on the bottom of the club head. If the contact is toward the toe or the heel, the lie angle of that particular club is not correct for you. The contact point should be in the center of the sole. An improper lie will produce off-line hits.

The type of shaft will be based upon your club head speed and what feels most comfortable to you. The higher your club head's speed—in other words, the farther you hit the ball—the firmer shaft you will want. If your swing speed is slow, you will want a more flexible shaft. Graphite shafts are lighter in weight, and I recommend them to almost all of my ladies. The lighter weight makes it easier to swing and easier to generate club head speed, because the total weight of the club is less.

Club head style will need to be determined. I recommend over-size irons, because they are often more forgiving, as well as perimeter weighting. Perimeter weighting means that the edges of the club head on the irons are thicker, which will help lessen missed shots. You will also need to determine if you are strong enough to swing the oversize woods. Often these are too big and uncomfortable to swing. Bigger is not always better, beyond a certain point.

The size of the golf grip should be such that as you close your left hand around the grip your fingers lightly touch the pad of your thumb. They should neither gap nor overlap.

If you go to a reputable club fitter, they will fit you out-of-doors, where you can see the flight of the ball. Do not trust that when you go to a retail store to buy clubs they are always what the salespeople say they are. The industry standards are improving because of public demand and I hope will continue to do so. My friends John and Tom at Osborne Golf at PGA National in

Florida have shown me what a difference properly fitted clubs can make on a daily basis in our golf schools.

Remember, "Clubs that fit better hit better." So invest the time to find out what is best for you.

Many of us do not address the issue of club fitting until later in our golf experience. I recommend you find a club fitter who can make you a set for a reasonable price. You also can keep in mind that you will probably not need a full set to get started.

When you start to play, you will probably find a few clubs that are your "favorites." For some reason, women seem to really lean toward the odd-numbered clubs, like the 9 iron, 7 iron, and 5 iron, most of the time forgetting that the even numbers exist. Oftentimes in my playing lesson I will suggest a club to a student and she will not even know that she owns that particular club, and there it is sitting right in the bag. When you start to play you do not need a full set of clubs unless you hit a really long ball. Often the difference between one club an the next, the 9 iron and 8 iron, for example, is not that large, so a full set may not be necessary.

The clubs you will need are as follows:

1. **A high-numbered wood, 7 for example. You could use this to tee off with as well as in the fairway.**

2. **Irons: 5 iron, 7 iron, and 9 iron. Many women have the even numbers and never use them anyway.**

3. **A pitching wedge and a sand wedge. You can use these to full-swing, but you will need both for your approach shots into the green.**

4. **A putter.**

So you can start quite successfully with only seven clubs. You and your professional can help you to determine what to add as you advance.

If you are trying to use a borrowed set or a hand-me-down set, please see that they are graphite shafted, perimeter weighted, and at least close to the proper length. If the clubs are slightly long, you can grip down lower on the grip of the club, but if they are too short, you should look into some new clubs.

Summary

You must address these issues during a fitting:

1. Club head style, size as well as whether the head is offset or not. Being offset will help slow club head speed to get the ball into the air.

2. Shaft flex and flex point: Slower club head speed will require a more flexible shaft as well as a lower kick point, which will both help the ball trajectory to be higher.

3. The length of the club.

4. Swing weight and overall weight: You need to find a balance between a club that is not too heavy in overall weight but still maintains the feeling of the swing weight and the club head awareness.

5. The lie of the club.

6. Grip size.

7. Driver length.

Lesson 25
Golf's Bottom Line— Cutting Costs

When you add it all up, golf can be very expensive. Here are some ways to save money and still enjoy the game.

1. Participate in Group Lessons or Clinics

By sharing your lesson time with others you can divide the cost. This can reduce your expense quite a bit. As the instructor moves from student to student you can work on any recommended changes. The instructor can keep his or her eye on you even if he or she is not directly working with you at that moment and make suggestions when necessary. With this method you will have to do some of the motivating yourself, because the instructor is not right there to watch your every move. Sharing lesson time with friends is also a great way to learn to help each other in the future. I really enjoy giving shared lessons. It is a lot of fun to share your lesson time with a friend. Not only will it allow you some down-time, to relax and clear your head, but it is also nice to have a person with whom you play some golf to help understand what you are working on. It is also nice when husbands and wives share their lessons, in most cases. This allows the husband to hear his wife and me work, to help avoid later confusion. I also find that a new student often feels more comfortable in the lesson situation with company.

2. Buy Used Golf Clubs or Knockoffs

Golf clubs are a lot like cars—the manufacturer changes the model every year so the consumer will desire the "better" set every year. This leaves a lot of used sets that are virtually brand-new. Your retail centers do not always advertise this, but if you ask around or watch in the newspaper you can often find a great set for a relatively inexpensive price. Do not agree right away on the price that is asked. They will normally be as happy to sell as you are to buy.

In the past I have always recommended name-brand clubs, but today the "knockoff" clubs are so good it is amazing. My only caution would be to make sure your supplier of these clubs has been around the area for a while and is reputable, so they will be around in the future if a club breaks or you have any other problems.

3. Buy Experienced Balls

You can purchase recycled golf balls at a much lower price than new balls. As a new golfer you will probably lose your share of golf balls, so a large investment in this area can be a mistake. There are many places to purchase these balls today, including the golf shop, the kid down the street, the car wash, and the department store in your area. My only caution is to make sure if they are supposed to be white they are, rather than a dingy beige or yellow. The off-white balls have been sitting in the water for too long and will not go as far as other balls when hit.

Try not to stress out every time you lose a ball. It is going to happen.

4. Play Public or Municipal Courses or Courses at Off-Peak hours or in a League

These are three great ways to cut costs. There are a lot of great public or municipal courses today, created because of a huge public demand. Many of them are very realistically priced. Public golf courses are my new found love. There are really some great public courses. The rules are usually less strict, so I can wear my sneakers and my comfortable clothes and do not have to worry about offending anyone. There is a small public course near where I live in Bridgehampton. It is a great little 9-hole course. The people who play there and the people who work there are as nice as can be. Every time I have been there, I have had a great time. Try a local public course, as long as it isn't super busy. I think you will like the more relaxed atmosphere.

Some courses offer greens fee reductions at nonpeak hours—usually late afternoons. Many courses will offer a reduced rate to league players as well. This is a great way to meet new people. Gary Player refers to golf as "a friend-making machine."

5. Walk—Carry Your Bag or Use a Pull Cart

You can save money as well as do yourself good if you walk rather than riding in a golf cart. Not all courses will allow this, so check in your area to find out who does, as well as any hours they may restrict walking.

It is fun and relaxing to walk and play a few holes in the

evening, when the course is usually less crowded as well as very peaceful. Make sure you have a light golf bag, not filled with ten thousand golf balls, which will totally load down a light golf bag.

There is something very peaceful about walking and carrying your own bag. Just take half of your clubs out of your bag and leave them in your car and take out some of the balls. You may find that you play better because the tempo of the game seems to flow. When I play with my father we almost always walk. This gives us a lot of quality time to talk and enjoy each other's company. Try walking sometimes.

6. Consider not Using a Golf Glove

A golf glove serves two purposes. First, it helps keep the club from slipping in your hands. Unless it is very warm, causing your hands to sweat, this may not be necessary. Second, it protects your hands from the roughness of the grip of the club. Your hands will toughen up over time, and you may find that as you develop calluses the glove is not necessary. In the meantime it might be a good idea to keep a couple of Band-Aids with you.

If you feel that a glove is necessary in your case, a synthetic all-weather glove will be less expensive than an all-leather glove, as well as lasting longer.

I used to always wear a glove, simply because it was the thing to do. I no longer wear a glove, and I don't miss it at all. Practice with and without and see which way you are more comfortable.

7. Use a Set of Less than 14 Clubs

As a new golfer you may find you do not use all of your clubs but lean toward three or four favorites. Ladies with less strength may find such a slight distance difference in between clubs that an entire set is not necessary.

The clubs you do need are a putter, a sand wedge, a pitching wedge, a wood to tee off with, and your choice of irons. Often a 9 iron, 7 iron, and 5 iron are plenty to get you started. You may when choosing a wood choose a high-numbered wood (5 or 7) you could use off the tee as well as on the fairway. You can always add clubs as you go.

Lesson 26
My Favorite Training Aids

Although there are a huge number of training aids out on the market today, I do not use a lot of them consistently. The training aids that I do use are usually very simple and most often things you already have.

When you are choosing a training aid, it *must* be specific to what you are trying to improve in *your* golf swing.

Here are my favorite training aids. Some you can buy, some you already have, and some you can make yourself.

1. A Weighted Golf Club

A weighted golf club will help develop your golf muscles as well as the width in your golf swing. The heaviness of the club should help you feel the club swing away from you. A weighted club is very beneficial in increasing strength, including hand and wrist strength. Be sure to also swing a lighter club so you can learn to increase your swing speed as well.

2. An Alignment Aid for Your Practice Time

You can use your golf clubs (be careful not to place the club so close that you accidentally strike and break it) or a painted two-by-four, or purchase a fancy painted and marked board to use as an alignment aid. I think you should always practice with an alignment aid. It will help you visually get used to how your body (hips, knees, and shoulders) as well as your feet should be positioned so you are properly aiming at your target. If your alignment is really poor, I would recommend you put an alignment aid on each side of the ball and look at where the line between the two aids is pointing so you know exactly where your target is.

Obviously you should not use these aids on the golf course, but the more you practice the proper position, the more likely you are to have proper alignment on the golf course.

3. The Left Arm Connector

The purpose of the left arm connector is to help coordinate the arms and the body as well as to promote a proper folding of the left arm on the forward swing, which would help a player keep from missing the ball to the right.

What I do not like about the connector is how it smushes the heck out of a woman's chest. I also felt a certain amount of self-consciousness about having it right over my chest. I do not like the double arm swing connectors due to the fact that they feel so restrictive.

My recommendation is that rather than buying this aid you just place a small towel or a golf glove under your left underarm and attempt to keep it in position during your golf swing. There should be no reason to lose width in your swing to keep the towel or golf glove in position as long as you have proper level rotation of your torso. Try this; it really works!!

I find head covers very helpful for women who tend to lift their arms in their backswing, rather than properly rotating. A new up-and-coming student of mine, Gale, just takes a couple of practice swings with a head cover and feels the proper motion that way. When she takes the head cover away, she is able to repeat the proper backswing and just kill the golf ball.

4. The Medicus (Hinge Club)

I think this is a fun club to try, but an expensive investment. I wish I had invented it. The purpose of the Medicus is to help with tempo and club face position at the top of your backswing. If you rush or jerk the club away from the ball in your take-away, the shaft will "break" alignment. It will also "break" alignment if your club face is not in a good position at the top of your back-swing. This would be a good aid for those who tend to hook (right to left curving of the ball) the ball because of a closed (pointing to the sky) club face at the top of their backswing. If you get good with the Medicus you should be able to hit golf balls successfully. This club is fun because it feels strange when the club hinges as you make a mistake: instant feedback. This is the goal of any good training aid, to tell you immediately if you are doing something incorrectly or correctly. If you are a slicer, I would not recommend this training aid.

5. A Putting Track

The purpose of a putting track is to help you repeat a putting stroke that will go straight back and straight through. This should help teach you to roll the ball on your intended target line. If your putter head gets off-line, it will hit the metal sides of the track, making a noise—instant feedback again.

A less expensive option, which you can purchase at any hardware store, is a chalk line. This is a carpenter's tool used to draw straight lines. Once you find a short, straight putt on the putting green you can snap a straight chalk line down on the ground and putt on the line. This will help you see the line of your putt and check your alignment (putter face and body) as well as practice stroking straight back and straight through. If your ball is getting off-line you can see at exactly what point this problem is occurring. The chalk line is also much more portable than a putting track. Both aids will help produce the same positive result.

You can also take two irons and lay them on the ground parallel to each other, so that the putter head just fits between the two shafts. This will allow you to practice making a straight back and straight through stroke, with no money invested.

6. The Golf Tee

I constantly use golf tees as a training aid. They are inexpensive and can produce instant feedback, as well as being very versatile.

You can place a tee in the ground in front of the ball and try to hit it with your club head. This will help you practice keeping the club head low enough to the ground in front of the ball so you can get the ball airborne.

You can also place the tee where you do *not* want your club head to go and try to avoid hitting the tee.

You can also place the smaller end of the tee between your pinkie and the grip of the club to check to see if you are keeping your fingers closed around the grip throughout the swing. I like using golf tees because they are readily available any time you need them.

7. The All Season Self-Improvement Swing Trainer (ASSIST)

The ASSIST is a weighted club with a fitted grip and an angular shaft and a yellow or blue rectangular head. I like this teaching aid because the fitted grip helps you practice getting your hands correctly on the club consistently. The weight in the club end helps you feel the club head swing, as well as develop your golf muscles. The angular shaft helps produce proper arm swing through the hitting area, producing club head swing.

I especially like this aid because the student uses it without hitting golf balls, so she can work on her golf swing not strictly tied to worrying about golf ball results.

8. A Mirror

A mirror on the driving range or in your home can help you check to see if what you think you are doing or what you want to do is what is actually happening. It can help you compare what you understand to be correct with what feels correct, which in many cases are different. It offers repetition with visual feedback. Practicing at home in front of a mirror also takes away worrying constantly what the golf ball is doing.

There are so many training aids today. Some are great and some are a waste of your money. Check with your professional to ensure that the training aids you use are good for you and worth your money. Training aids can be used to help make a change in your golf swing that you are unable to make on your own.

My students sometimes dread their training aids. They are oftentimes not the most comfortable. Do not look at your training aid as a punishment but a means to an end. I am not trying to make you uncomfortable, but to help you to be a better golfer. If your instructor recommends a training aid or a practice drill, realize that it is to help you and to decrease the amount of time it takes you to make the necessary change.

Lesson 27
How to Play Faster

You will not be able to play faster unless you are taught how. Your speed will improve over time, as will your golf game in general, if you continue to work on it.

You must keep the pace of play up, or you will be virtually run off the golf course, by either the ranger or the other golfers. The average-length hole should take no more than 15 minutes. Less for par 3s: 12 minutes or less. Slightly more for par 5s: no more than 18 minutes.

You may forgo keeping score in exchange for keeping time. Note the time at which you tee off on the scorecard, and calculate the time at which you should finish the hole. Keep an eye on your watch, and if you have not completed the hole by that time, immediately pick up the ball and progress to the next tee. In the long run you will appreciate having learned this valuable lesson.

When I ran the nine-holers, they had time restrictions. When they teed off on each hole, they would write down the time they started and note the time they should finish the hole. If they had not finished the hole by this time, they were to pick up their golf ball and move to the next hole. They learned to play very quickly. By the end of the first season they could easily complete nine holes in two hours. Try this system with your group. It really works. Many of these ladies have now graduated to 18-holers and are doing quite well.

Suggestions for Playing Faster

Play ready golf, which means being ready to hit when it is your turn, including glove on, club in hand, practice swing completed, and target already picked.

Take plenty of golf balls with you. Looking for golf balls is very time-consuming. After marking where the ball landed, if you cannot find it within one minute move on.

Walk a bit faster than you are accustomed to. I often see ladies slowly sauntering down the fairway, as if modeling in a fashion show. Pick up those feet, and keep it moving. If you move quickly between shots, you will not need to rush your shot when you get there.

When you bring clubs with which to chip or pitch to the putting green, be sure to leave them on the side of the green where you will exit to the next hole. Be sure to leave your clubs where you can clearly see them. Do not set them into the longer grass where they could easily be forgotten. You may also want to put name labels on your clubs in case this happens. Leaving them on the opposite side will mean a huge waste of your time and energy.

Line up your putts while you are waiting for others to putt, as long as you don't stand in their line of vision as they're putting. Repair ball marks on the green while you are waiting for others to putt. Replace divots on the fairway as you are waiting for others to hit.

Take several clubs with you to your next shot, so you will not have to return to your bag because you guessed the wrong club.

If you are playing golf in a cart with a partner, park the cart in between your two golf balls and each of you walk to your ball.

When you are around the green hitting your approach, always take your putter with you to avoid having to return to the cart again.

When parking the cart, always park even with or past the green, so that you do not have to walk backward toward the fairway, which will hold up players behind you.

Please do not waste time putting your head covers on after each shot. Take the covers off before your tee off, keep them in the basket in the cart until you are finished with your round, and then replace them on your clubs.

Consider playing in twosomes or threesomes rather than foursomes. With fewer players in the group, you should be able to move quicker.

Play during nonpeak hours. Playing a few holes in the evening will help you feel more comfortable, because there will probably be fewer players on the course.

Organize your clubs in your golf bag properly. Believe it or not, there is a proper place for your clubs to be placed in your bag. This will make it quicker and easier to locate your club of choice when it is your turn to hit. The higher side of the bag will hold the physically longer clubs, the woods, the middle height of the bag will contain the long irons, such as the 4, 5, 6, and 7 irons, and the lowest side of the bag will contain the physically shortest clubs, such as the wedges and 9 and 8 iron. The putter can go either high or low. If you know where your clubs are in the bag, it will save you the embarrassment of fumbling through your bag to find a club every time.

Also, limit the number of practice swings.

Learn from watching others. Do not look on playing with better players as intimidating but as an opportunity to learn. Observe their timesaving habits and try to mimic them. With a little practice, you will play quicker, which will allow you, as well as the other golfers around you, to enjoy the game more.

Lesson 28
Playing in Ladies' Day

You've decided you want to play in ladies' day. My first question is, "Are you crazy?" Now, I'm just kidding. Ladies' day has numerous positives and few pitfalls, about which I am here to forewarn you.

I ran ladies' day for a lot of years. There were many positives for the ladies involved. For example, meeting new people, the camaraderie of playing in a team event, learning different types of tournaments, and enjoying the fancy member guests and just the game in general.

To play in ladies' day you will probably need an established 18-hole handicap. You can check on this when you sign up for your ladies' golf association. Check with one of your golf professionals on how to join. You will be charged a fee. This fee normally goes toward the weekly running of the events as well as the prize fund.

Once you are a member of the association, you will need to sign up for each weekly event. Sign up promptly, and be considerate of others and sure to cancel if you cannot make the event. This makes it easier on your professional staff, who are forced to juggle the pairings if you do not show up, as well as those you were scheduled to play.

The sign-up sheet should list the format of the tournament and the tee-off time. Be responsible and sign up for yourself. This will avoid the disappointment when your friend has forgotten to sign you up and you arrive to play and cannot. Every week when I ran ladies' day, several ladies would show up who were positive they had signed up. I would then pull out the sign-up sheet, and on occasion it had been my mistake, but more often than not they had forgotten to sign up or had signed up on the wrong sheet.

You need to have a working knowledge of the rules of the game at this point. If you do not, you are setting yourself up to be attacked by the rules shark. Every club has several of them. Avoid this potential embarrassment by familiarizing yourself with the rules book and its layout. Also, be sure to carry one in your bag. Refer to the book every time you have a question. Many ladies will act like they know the rules but do not. I have played golf my entire life and do not claim to know all of the rules, not even close. I *always* refer to my rules book when I have or am asked a question.

On the day of the tournament be sure to arrive early enough to check in to receive your scorecard, pairing for the tournament, and rules sheet. Be sure to read the rules sheet. This will provide you with the necessary information for the day, including the format and any special rules you will need to know. You will also want enough time to be able to hit a few balls to warm up, as well as the time to meet the ladies you are playing with whom you may not already know.

You will probably play in a shotgun start, which means the

entire field starts at the same time on different holes. This will allow the field to finish at approximately the same time.

If you are keeping score, be sure to check your playing partners' score after each hole. If you are not keeping the official scorecard, it is a good idea to keep your own score on a separate card, just to keep track in case there are any questions at the end. If you have trouble remembering your own score on each hole, I highly recommend you purchase one of those bead counters you can attach to your belt loop. It isn't necessarily the coolest-looking accessory, but it is a *huge* improvement over being suspected of shaving strokes off your score. When I was running ladies' day at Admirals Cove, every other week at least one woman would complain to me that someone in her group had not counted all of her strokes. I would like to believe that in 99 percent of these cases they just truly forgot the strokes. But if you are not careful, this negative perception will precede you.

You also must be able to keep pace with the group. If you are having a bad hole and it is a team competition, you should pick up your golf ball and put it into your pocket, as long as someone on your team is in the hole to carry the team. The hard part here is that slow players do not realize they are slow.

A local club in my area started this terrible program, in my opinion, called Sally Slow Play. I just believe that the ladies in charge of this lost sight of the human element and what is most important—people's feelings. If a group was out of position, they were forced to pick up their golf balls and move to the next hole. This I can understand; however, they posted a sticker with a turtle on the scoreboard by their names in front of the entire field. This was unfair to those in the group who were not the problem. Rather than going directly to the person in the group who was the problem, they made a spectacle of the others as well. This can be the harsh reality of ladies' day. So be ready for it.

Once you finish your round you should tally your scorecard

and make sure that there are also two signatures on the card. Be sure to thank the ladies you had the opportunity to play with, and also thank your professional staff, who are working very hard so that you enjoy your day.

Ladies' day can be a very positive experience, but keep in mind it isn't always "Pleasantville."

Lesson 29

Are Women People in the World of Golf?

It is still amazing to me that in today's world there are still so many restrictions on women in golf. To a certain extent it infuriates me. My husband, Tim, thinks it best not to bring up the topic with me. There are still all-male golf clubs in the United States that will not even allow women in the gate. This is crazy. I do not wish my husband to play at any club that will not allow me to play. There are still golf clubs in the United States that will only allow women to be members if their husband dies. This is ridiculous!!

The good news is that it is getting better. Not better enough, but better. Atlantic Golf Club, where I currently have the privilege to work in the summer in Bridgehampton, New York, has several of their memberships in which the woman is the primary member. Also, many of the tournaments are open to both men and women. This gender-neutral attitude makes a lot more sense to me. We have got to continue to work toward equality.

Many golf clubs have tee times restricted according to sex. This is preposterous. In the olden days, when many men worked while women stayed home, I could maybe understand the reasoning behind this idea. Times have changed. Many women work. Why should we be restricted to certain tee times and excluded from others? If tee times were restricted based upon handicap, I could totally understanding restricting the times in the busy hours to the better golfers. This, unfortunately, is not always the measure of whether they will play quickly. There are plenty of good golfers who are deathly slow. This could also potentially help reduce the sandbagger problem of the golfers who elevate their handicaps intentionally in order to win golf tournaments. If you are a member of a golf club in which you can be involved with the rule making, work hard to abolish restricted tee times that are based upon sex.

I remember playing a round of golf at a club in Pittsburgh with a friend of mine from college who was from there. We arrived at the club and went into the pro shop to check in. The golf professional then informed us that we would have to wait one and one-half hours to tee off because when my friend called he did not realize that I was a woman and women were not allowed to tee off until after noon. To say the very least, I was not happy. I ventured out to the first tee to watch the men tee off. As each one of them stepped up to the tee, making his less than perfect golf swing, I progressively got even angrier. I could have beaten each of these guys with a blindfold on. This was just a rule that didn't make any sense. I am very good at following rules that make sense, but when they don't I tend to get myself in trouble. Oh, well!

Now that I am off my soapbox, I'll tell you how to deal with the men who believe that golf is not a game for women. There are a lot of them, by the way. Besides your very obvious chauvinists, there are a lot of closet chauvinists. In order to have any credibility as a woman in the golf world, you must attain a certain level of skill and, probably more important, the ability to play very quickly! This is crucial. If you join the men on the golf course on Saturday and Sunday mornings and play slowly, you are ruining the reputation of women in golf. You must play 18 holes of golf in four hours or less. Due to very poor stereotyping, women have and probably will continue to have the reputation of playing slowly. And by the way, many women *are* slow. There are also a lot of men who are slow as well.

When you progressively enter the world of the popular tee time hours you must handle yourself appropriately. Do *not* allow the men to bully you. If you have the 9:00 tee time and a group of men drive up with the 9:10 tee time and ask to tee off ahead of you, do *not* let them go. After you tee off on the first tee, you must keep up with the group ahead of you. If you are lagging behind, pick up your golf balls and move ahead. If you find you continually have to do this, you do not play quickly enough and should probably not be playing during the busy hours. You must earn respect for yourself by acting and behaving as if you belong there. Until you are comfortable with your golf and your ability to play quickly, do *not* put yourself in the middle of the busiest time. You can earn your comfort in the busiest times, when you have had more experience and success.

We must stick together to earn respect as well as equality. I think we can do it!

I Never Did Find the Women's Grill

I had the privilege in the summer of 1993 of playing a private country club in Philadelphia with an incredibly beautiful course as well as clubhouse. The names have been deleted to protect the innocent, if there are any. I truly was lost trying to find the ladies' locker room in an effort to change for dinner to celebrate my birthday and accidentally walked right into the men's grill, which was filled with cigar smoke and several tables surrounded with old men playing cards. You would have thought I was trying to steal the Hope diamond. Oh, my God! A woman in the men's grill. What a travesty. The reaction, or overreaction, was amazing. To make a long story short, I was quickly kicked out. It amazes me that this situation exists. Many clubs today are making additions of men's grills. Just in case you do not know what a men's grill is, it is a men-only room, often connected to the men's locker room, where the male members can sit around in their underwear, drink, smoke, play cards, and whatever, where women are definitely not invited or welcome. Once again, I could accept this if there were a women's grill. I looked for one, but I just couldn't find it. Separate but equal would be much more acceptable.

We must stick together to achieve the equality we deserve.

The Good News

There are clubs that will allow women as members. Most of the new clubs being built today have adopted a more gender-neutral attitude. If you can afford the cost of membership, many of the new clubs will accept you. You will have to do a little research, but I hope your time will be rewarded with a golf membership and hours of fun. If you cannot afford to be a member of a private club, public courses as well as daily fee courses should not have any restrictions based upon gender.

Where We Stand Legally

There are numerous lawsuits pending where women are suing golf clubs based upon preferential treatment toward their male counterparts. Laws have been passed in several states that require country clubs to provide equal access if the club conducts outside business, such as outings. This is only a start to making the situation better. It will take time, but things are getting better.

Many clubs have bylaws that restrict memberships to men or exclude women from serving on the club's governing body. This is where I believe most of our problems are stemming from. I would be interested to know what percentage of clubs in the United States do not have a woman member. Too many, I am sure. Keep up the fight toward equality.

Last but not least, here is the most ridiculous policy I have heard. Suppose a husband and wife are members of a club for 30 years. Unfortunately, the husband passes away. The wife may not be given the rights of membership anymore. We must define ourselves individually, not by that of our husband.

Lesson 30
Watching Golf on Television

While you may not think of a televised golf tournament as educational, for a beginner golfer it certainly can be. Golf lingo is a language of its own. Part of being a true golfer is being able to sound like a golfer. The glossary at the end of this book will help you with this process.

You will learn from television that good golf swings appear effortless; the game looks easy. Try not to be deceived. Good golf swings look easy because they are rhythmic and there are no extraneous motions. Also, keep in mind the thousands of hours that the golfer put in to get to this point.

It is also important to understand that when you are watching an LPGA or PGA tournament on television you are seeing the best golfers in the world, playing their best. Also, the telecast often shows only the best shots. They flash away to a player making a putt for birdie. I would also like to see some of the guys or girls who are struggling to make the cut, as well as a few of the missed shots. In my opinion, television gives us a false sense of what we can expect when we play golf.

TOURNAMENT TELECAST TERMS

A cell: A thunderstorm, which will show up as a roundish cell on a radar return.

A flier: A ball hit out of the rough, in which the grass gets between the ball and club face, reducing or eliminating spin, so the ball flies farther than usual.

A lot of green to work with: Much distance between the edge of the green and the cup, so the player has adequate space in which to hit an approach.

Amateur: A person who plays golf only for the love of it and not for payment or for deferment of his or her expenses.

A peg under it: Teed up.

A tester: A difficult putt.

Back bunker: A bunker in the back of the green.

Back fringe: The apron surrounding the edge of the green; in this case, it would be the grass encircling the back of the green.

Bubble driver: A driver with a bulge in the shaft.

Choking up on: Gripping down on a club, so that the ball goes a shorter distance than it would using the full shaft length.

Chunk: To hit the ball fat or to take too much turf with the shot, often before the ball.

Collar starts tightening: A player is becoming excessively nervous.

Collection area: A low point on a hole where excessive water collects and golf balls tend to roll.

Costly bogey: One over par on a hole, occurring at a disadvantageous time in a tournament.

Cross handed grip: A grip used in putting in which the left hand is placed lower on the grip than the right, also called a left-hand low grip.

Dance floor: The putting green.

Duck hook: A low curving shot from right to left.

Environmentally sensitive area: An area set aside to protect it.

Even: Even with par.

Finishing hole: The last hole on the course.

Got one club length: When relief is granted, as from casual water or an obstruction, the relief is one club length.

Ham 'n' egged it: When two partners in a competition's scores on separate holes compensated for each other. Or when one partner did badly on a hole on which her partner did well.

Hard wedge: A full, hard swing with a pitching or a sand wedge.

Hit it right through the break: To hit the putt so hard it did not respond to the slope in the green.

In-between clubs: Shots of a yardage that does not fit into the distance a player normally hits a club.

Inside the hole: Aiming within the cup, playing little or no break.

Intermediate cut: The second cut of rough in from the fairway.

Jump all over it: To hit the ball extraordinarily hard.

Knock it inside (another player's ball): To hit a ball closer to the pin on the green than the other player's ball.

Knock the ball down: To intentionally hit the ball lower, to avoid the effects of the wind.

Leader in the clubhouse: The player who has the lowest par of all who have completed their rounds.

Left it out: Hit a push, without any compensating hook, where the ball ends up too far to the right of the target.

Left to right: A green that slopes from left to right, causing the putt to break or curve in that direction.

Little green to work with: A very short distance between the edge of the green and the cup.

Lose the ball to the right: To hit a push or a slice.

Made the cut: Shot a low-enough score to qualify for the last two days' play.

Maneuver the ball: To cause an intentional slice or hook on the ball to go around an obstruction.

Misread it (a putt): Make an incorrect diagnosis of the break on the green.

Missed the cut: Failed to shoot a low-enough score to qualify for the last two days' play.

Never had a chance: When a putt is left very short of the hole or seriously off-line, so that it never would have gone in.

On top of: When one player in a group has sunk a putt and the next player sinks one immediately after.

Over: More than par.

Playing on an exemption: When tournament sponsors are privileged to grant entry exemptions to players who did not qualify by usual methods.

Poa annua: A grassy weed that often invades putting greens and disrupts the consistency of the green.

Pot bunkers: Small, round bunkers, often seen on European courses.

Ripped sand wedge: A sand wedge hit very hard.

Primary rough: The rough adjacent to the fairway, usually longer in length.

Preferred lies: Played when course conditions are poor. Players are allowed to lift the ball, clean it, and replace it within a specified distance in an improved lie.

Solid hit: A well-hit ball.

Solid round of golf: Round of golf in which a player hits the ball well throughout the entire round.

Some holes left: Several holes remaining before the completion of a round.

Spin it: To put backspin on the ball, causing it to stop quickly.

The cut: In most tournaments, when the field is cut in half after the first two rounds. The lowest scorers make the cut and qualify for the last two days of play.

The green goes away from you: The green slopes away from the player, so that the front is higher than the back, often making it difficult to stop the ball on the green.

The nineteenth hole: The bar.

They're on the clock: Officials are timing a group because of their slow play.

Titanium: A very strong lightweight metal, now being used in golf club manufacturing.

Under: Below par

Up and down: To hit an approach and putt the ball into the cup in one more shot.

Use the loft of the club: To exploit the angle of the club face to hit a high shot.

As you progress in your learning experience, you will slowly pick up these terms. Watching golf on television can help you pick up the lingo quicker. Also, make sure to watch the golfers' course management skills, often hitting irons off the tee on the par 4s and par 5s to ensure keeping the ball on the fairway.

Lesson 31
Playing Pregnant—To Swing or Not to Swing?

Congratulations! You're having a baby. Should your golf game have to suffer? Well, the good news is that the answer is no. With a few adjustments in your setup and your expectations, you can play as long as your doctor sees fit.

To accommodate your growing belly, you will want to bend over more forward from your hips at your setup position, to give yourself the ability to swing your arms. You may also find when you putt that you have to place the putter farther away from you to avoid the putter tangling in your clothing.

More important are the health concerns. Drink plenty of fluids, water being the liquid of choice. Eight glasses daily is minimal. Also, put nutritious snacks in your golf bag, the kind that won't melt down into an indistinguishable blob. You may also add more fruit juice to your diet. You will want to avoid playing in the heat of the day. Playing early in the morning or later in the evening may help accommodate this. You will want to limit the number of holes you play to the point at which you are tired, even if it is not nine holes. If you are tired after six, quit after six. You will want to take a cart with you to make this easier.

You will want to wear loose, but not too loose, clothing. This will allow you to be comfortable but keep your clothing from tangling with the clubs. Most maternity clothing will not have pockets, so be prepared to keep a couple of tees and balls in the cart close to you. You may also find that as your feet swell you are more comfortable in a pair of loose-fitting sneakers rather than your golf shoes.

Many women have found that their golf improves during their pregnancy. While I was playing a tournament series in Australia, another professional who was seven and one-half months pregnant played quite a bit better than I did. My friend Kathy Hart Wood recently shot a fine score of 73 at eight and one-half months pregnant. Pretty impressive, pregnant or not. So get out your clubs and keep swinging!

Lesson 32

What Is a Handicap, and How Do I Get One?

The handicap system allows players of differing abilities to play against each other on a level playing field. If I were a very high handicapped player (a beginner), this system would allow me to play equally against a very advanced, low handicapped player.

How Is a Handicap Computed?

A very simple answer to this very complicated formula is that your handicap is a percentage of your lowest scores relative to par. So, very, very roughly, if you turned in five scores of 110, 122, 115, 118, and 112, the system would accept the better scores and ignore the higher scores. So the system would accept the 110 and the 112. The system would then compare these scores to the course rating (a rating based upon the difficulty of the course, usually just slightly lower or higher than the par). The difference between the two would be your handicap. Example: If 111 is your average score, subtract the course rating, 70.0 for example, to get a 41 handicap.

What Is a Handicap Index?

A handicap index is a handicap with a decimal in it, for example, 34.6 or 40.5, which allows you to take your index to another course and plug it into their chart to give you the appropriate handicap for that course based upon difficulty. This allows you to have a handicap that is fair at any course you play. If you were to play a more difficult course, you would receive more strokes than you normally would, and if you were to play an easier course, you would receive fewer strokes.

Questions and Answers

Question: I cannot complete every hole. I have a couple of bad holes every round, and I pick up the ball to keep play moving. Can I still establish a handicap?

Answer: Yes. On the holes where you pick up your ball, score the maximum score of 11 on your scorecard, unless you realistically think your score would have been lower. For example, suppose you were on the green in six and you picked up. You realistically would probably not have scored worse than a nine. So record a nine.

Question: How many scores do I need to turn in to establish a handicap?

Answer: You will need to turn in five eighteen-hole scores to establish a handicap.

Question: I do not have time to play 18 holes. Can I turn in my 9-hole scores?

Answer: Yes and no. First, do not attempt to post your 9-hole scores in the handicap computer. They could potentially be high enough as a beginner that the computer accepts them as 18-hole scores. A woman at a club where I worked in Florida did this and ended up with a plus two handicap (a very, very low handicap). Very often your club will allow you to combine two 9-hole scores to produce an 18-hole score.

Very recently it is acceptable to post 9-hole scores. Check with your golf professional.

Question: What is the maximum handicap?

Answer: The individual club determines this. The maximum handicap may be 44 or 36. But some clubs will allow the handicap to be as high as it may be. Keep in mind that there may be a limit for tournament play, however. A new golfer at Atlantic started out with a 56 handicap. She is now in the low thirties. This is quite an accomplishment.

Please do not post only your good scores. Post all of your scores. My friend Amy would only post her lowest scores. She did not realize that the computer would disregard her high scores and ended up with a handicap that was too low for her. From what I have seen, women seem to be exactly the opposite from men when it comes to handicap. We seem to attach more importance to having the lower handicap, whether we can play to it or not. The men like to slightly pad their handicap so that it is a little higher than it may be in reality, so they are covered when they play for money.

Keep in mind that you should only play to your handicap when you play well. Your best scores determine your handicap. If you play to your handicap or better all the time, you are not posting your scores. When I was a junior golfer at Seneca Lake Country Club, I could not wait to post my scores, especially when I played well. There was an older lady at the club who would never post her scores, especially when she played well. Therefore, her handicap was falsely high and she would win all of the net tournaments. This would drive me as well as a lot of other members crazy. So, I took matters into my own hands and posted her scores for her every time I played with her. This was probably not the right thing for me to do, but it sure was fun. Now this was in the olden days, when you posted your scores with pencil and paper. I would come in the next day to find out that she had erased the score that I had posted for her. So she and I would play this juvenile game of cat and mouse. I don't know if she ever stopped being a sandbagger, but it sure was fun trying to play the game with her. Still, this was something the golf committee should have been taking care of, not a junior golfer.

Question: What is the handicap row on the scorecard for?

Answer: If you look at a scorecard, you will see a row that lists the handicapping of the holes. This is basically a rating of the holes from 1 to 18 in order of difficulty, 1 being the most difficult and 18 being the easiest. The handicapping of the holes allows you to determine for which holes you will receive your strokes. For example, if I am a 2 handicap and you are a 21 handicap, I need to give you 19 strokes (21 minus 2). If we play match play (hole-by-hole competition), I need to give you 19 strokes. With 1 on every hole, 19 strokes minus 18 holes leaves 1 leftover. Where do you receive that extra stroke? On the

most difficult hole, the number-one rated hole. So, you would receive two strokes on this one hole and one on the rest.

When you start playing and you feel that you can actually come close to keeping score I recommend that you attempt to establish a handicap as quickly as possible. This is always a good measurement to recognize your improvement. It will also show you the importance of the short game when it comes to scoring. You may start to hit the ball much better, but your scores, therefore your handicap, will not come down until your short game is respectable.

Conclusion

Part Three

Conclusion

I hope I have helped to answer some of your questions. Keep everything as simple as possible. If what you are doing is working, do not question it, but enjoy. If what you are doing is not working, find your professional for a couple key ideas to work on and stick with them. Have fun with your learning experience. Trust your professional, and work hard. The more you put into your golf game, the more you will get out of your golf game. Be patient. Gaining a good working knowledge of the game should take an average of about five years. This should be a fun time. Have fun and smile!

Glossary

Part Four

Glossary

Part of becoming a true golfer is sounding like a golfer. Your lingo alone can define your level of ability. Listen to other golfers speak, and have your professional help you with this as well.

Address: The way you position your body in relation to the club and to the ball.

Alignment: The position in which you set your body to control the direction of the ball.

Away: The person who is "away" is farthest from the target and will be the first to play the next shot.

Balata: A soft material for golf ball covering that helps lower handicapped players in an effort to get the ball to stop rolling quicker.

Best ball: A tournament where a determined number of the best score of the team on each hole counts as the score for the team. For example, one best ball of two or two best balls of four.

Birdie: Scoring one shot less than par on an individual hole.

Bite: When the ball stops rolling quickly.

Blading: Hitting high on the ball, causing it to go low and run rather than get into the air. Also called hitting the ball thin, skulling, or topping the ball.

Bogey: One stroke more than par on an individual hole.

Break: The curving of the ball on the putting surface caused by undulations.

Bunker: A sand- or grass-filled indentation in the ground.

Chili dip: Hitting the ground before the ball, normally causing the ball to go a shorter distance than planned. Also called chunk, fat, or hitting behind the ball.

Chip: A shot of relatively short distance, hit with no wrist movement, in an effort to get the ball onto the putting surface as close to the hole as possible.

Chip and run: A chip hit with a less lofted club or more in line with the back foot, producing a less lofted shot with more roll.

Chunk: Hitting the ground before the ball, normally causing the ball to go a shorter distance than planned. Also called fat, hitting behind the ball, or chili dip.

Closed face: The club face aiming left of the intended target line in relation to the line of your feet.

Closed stance: Body or line of feet aiming to the right of the target rather than parallel to target line. Stomach faces away from the target more.

Course rating: A number computed based upon the difficulty of the course, necessary to figure out handicap.

Cup: The plastic lining in the putting green where the flagstick is inserted.

Cut shot: A small curvature of the ball from left to right for a right-handed player. A small slice. Also called a fade.

Divot: A chunk of turf removed from the ground with the club head in a swing.

Dogleg: A severe change in direction to the right or left on a hole.

Draw: A small curvature of the ball from right to left for a right-handed player. A small hook.

Drive: The first shot hit from each teeing ground.

Driver: The 1 wood.

Duck hook: A very severe curvature from right to left of the ball for a right-handed player. A large hook.

Eagle: Two strokes less than par on an individual hole. For example, a one on a par 3, a two on a par 4, or a three on a par 5.

Fade: A small curvature of the ball from left to right for a right-handed player. Also called a cut shot.

Fairway: The closely mown area between the teeing area and the putting surface.

Fairway bunker: A bunker greater than approximately 30 yards away from the green.

Fat: Hitting the ground before the ball, normally causing the ball to go a shorter distance than anticipated. Also called a chunk, hitting behind the ball, or chili dip.

Flagstick: The flag and pin placed into the cup or hole on the putting surface of each hole. Also called the pin.

Fore: What you should yell if your ball is heading where it could possibly hit another person.

Foursome: Most commonly a group of four players, normally the maximum number of players allowed to play together.

Fried egg: A ball buried in the sand of a bunker.

Fringe: The slightly longer cut of grass surrounding the putting surface. Also called the apron.

"Gimme" or a putt that is "good": A short putt conceded by an opponent. Not legal in stroke play.

Green: The closely mown surface that contains the cup and flagstick. Also called the putting surface.

Greens fee: The amount charged to play a golf course. Often does not include the cart charge.

Green side bunker: A sand area surrounding the green or putting surface.

Gross score: The actual shot on a hole or round before handicap is subtracted.

Handicap: The number of strokes you can subtract from your gross or total score, computed by taking a percentage of your best scores. The handicapping of the holes is a ranking of the holes in order of difficulty, ranging from 1 to 18. The handicap system allows players of different abilities to compete on an equal basis.

Handicap index: A traveling handicap that allows you to plug your number into the course chart to convert your handicap to an appropriate handicap for that course.

Hazard: A yellow- or red-staked area, including sand bunkers.

Hitting behind the ball: Hitting the ground before the ball, normally causing the ball to go a shorter distance than planned. Also called chunk, fat, or chili dip.

Hitting the ball thin: Hitting high on the ball, causing it to go low and run rather than get into the air. Also called blading, a skull, or topping the ball.

Honor: The player with the "honor" is the person who has the right to tee off first on the next hole by scoring best on the last hole. If there is a tie, the order remains as it was on the previous hole. If you are playing ready golf, this is sometimes ignored.

Hook: A severe curvature of the ball from right to left for a right-handed player, left to right for a left-handed player.

Lag putt: A putt intended to just get the ball close to the hole.

Lateral hazard: An area marked with red stakes or lines.

Lie: The position in which the ball sits on the ground.

Lip: The front edge of the bunker.

Loft: The angle upward of the club face. Also the height or trajectory of a shot.

Match play: A competition between two players or teams decided by the team winning the most holes, each hole worth only one point.

Medal play: A competition based on the player with the fewest total strokes winning. Also called stroke play.

Mulligan: A second try after an unsuccessful attempt. Not legal.

Net score: Gross or actual score minus your handicap.

Open face: A club face aiming to the right of the intended target line.

Open stance: The line of the feet aiming to the left of the target for a right-handed player. Stomach faces more toward target.

Out-of-bounds: An area marked with white stakes from which you are not allowed to play the ball, penalty being stroke and distance.

Par: The score an expert golfer is expected to make on a hole under normal conditions allowing two putts.

Pin: The flag and pin placed into the cup or hole on the putting surface of each hole. Also called the flagstick.

Pitch: A lofted shot, smaller than a full swing, intended to get the ball up and close to the pin. Bigger than a chip and smaller than a full swing.

Pitching wedge: A 10 iron.

Plugged ball: A ball embedded in the ground.

Preferred lies: Rules that when in effect allow players to lift, clean, and place the ball within a predetermined length from where the ball lies no closer to the hole, provided the ball originally lies in the fairway of the hole you are playing. Also called winter rules.

Provisional ball: An extra ball hit from the original area where the ball lay, in an effort to save time, in case the ball originally hit is lost or out-of-bounds.

Pull: A shot that goes left of the target line with no curvature for a right-handed player.

Push: A shot that goes right of the target line with no curvature for a right-handed player.

Putting: The rolling of the ball in an effort to get the ball into the cup with a club designed with little or no loft.

Putting surface: The closely mown surface that contains the cup and flatstick. Also called the green.

Rough: The area to the sides of the fairway, with longer grass.

Sand wedge: An 11 iron, a club with a lot of loft. Hits ball high with less roll.

Scramble tournament: A team tournament in which all players teeing off choose the best shot and then hit from there. This process continues until the ball is holed, including putts.

Scratch golfer: A golfer with a zero handicap.

Shank: A shot hit out of the neck or hosel of the club, causing the ball to go severely right and often low.

Shotgun start: The method by which groups start on different holes at the same time, therefore finishing at the same time.

Skull: Hitting high on the ball, causing it to go low and run rather than get into the air. Also called blading or hitting the ball thin, or topping the ball.

Slice: A ball curving severely from left to right for a right-handed player.

Slope: A number based upon the difficulty of the golf course, necessary to compute handicap. Different for each set of tees.

Spikes: Golf shoes.

Sky: To hit the ball extremely high, causing a loss in distance. Noun: pop-up.

Stroke play: A competition based on the player with the fewest total strokes winning. Also called medal play.

Surilyn: A hard material used to cover a golf ball recommended for new players promoting distance and durability.

Take-away: The first two feet of the club moving away from the ball initially.

Target line: An imaginary line extended through the ball to the target.

Tee: The peg on which the ball is placed for the first shot of each hole. Also the area from which you hit your first shot of each hole.

Tee shot: The first shot on each hole.

Tee time: A time assigned at which you may play the course.

Tempo: The pace of the swing.

Threesome: Three players in a group.

Topping the ball: Hitting high on the ball, causing it to go low and run rather than get into the air. Also called blading, a skull, or hitting the ball thin.

Twosome: Two players in a group.

Unplayable lie: A position in which the ball sits where the player opts to take a penalty stroke in order to move the position of the ball within two club lengths no closer to the hole.

Up and down: Taking one chip and one putt to get the ball into the hole.

Whiff: To swing and miss the ball completely. Not the end of the world.

Winter rules: Rules that when in effect allows players to lift, clean, and place the ball within a predetermined length from where the ball lies no closer to the hole, provided the ball originally lies in the fairway of the hole you are playing. Also called preferred lies.